Designs
for
Learning

Designs *for* Learning

A New Architecture for Professional Development in Schools

Paul V. Bredeson

CORWIN PRESS, INC.
A Sage Publications Company
Thousand Oaks, California

For information:

Corwin Press, Inc.
A Sage Publications Company
2455 Teller Road
Thousand Oaks, California 91320
www.corwinpress.com

Sage Publications Ltd.
6 Bonhill Street
London EC2A 4PU
United Kingdom

Sage Publications India Pvt. Ltd.
M-32 Market
Greater Kailash I
New Delhi 110 048 India

Printed in the United States of America

Library of Congress Cataloging-in-Publication Data

Bredeson, Paul V.
Designs for learning : a new architecture for professional development / Paul V. Bredeson.
    p. cm.
Includes bibliographical references and index.
ISBN 0-7619-7889-5 (C) — ISBN 0-7619-7890-9 (P)
    1. Teachers-In-service training-United States. 2. Continuing education-United States.
I. Title.
LB1731 .B724 2003
370'.71'5—dc21

                                                2002015584

This book is printed on acid-free paper.

01 02 03 04 05 10 9 8 7 6 5 4 3 2 1

Acquisitions Editor:	Rachel Livsey
Editorial Assistant:	Phyllis Cappello
Copy Editor:	Jon Preimesberger
Production Editor:	Sanford Robinson
Typesetter:	C&M Digitals (P) Ltd.
Proofreader:	Toni Williams
Indexer:	Teri Greenberg
Cover Designer:	Michael Dubowe
Production Artist:	Michelle Lee

This book is dedicated to my grandchildren,
Kyra Ann and Maxwell Dean, and their future teachers.

Contents

List of Tables and Figures — xii

Preface — xv

About the Author — xxiii

PART I   REDESIGNING PROFESSIONAL LEARNING FOR EDUCATORS — 1

1. **Breaking the Box: New Designs for Professional Learning in Schools** — 3
    Introduction — 3
    Thinking Outside and Beyond the Box — 5
    Utilitas, Firmitas, and Venustas:
        Essential Components of Architecture — 5
        Function (Utilitas) — 5
        Structure (Firmitas) — 6
        Beauty (Venustas) — 7
    Professional Development Design Themes — 7
        Design Theme One—Professional Development
            Is About Learning — 9
        Design Theme Two—Professional Development Is Work — 9
        Design Theme Three—Professional Expertise
            Is a Journey, Not a Credential — 10
        Design Theme Four—Opportunities for Professional
            Learning That Informs Practice Are Unbounded — 11
        Design Theme Five—Student Learning, Professional
            Development, and Organizational Mission Are
            Intimately Related — 11

Design Theme Six—Professional Development
Is About People, Not Programs 12
Why Is It Important to Redesign Professional
Development in Schools? 12
Changing the Paradigm of Professional Development 16

2. **Building Beneath the Surface: Footings and
Foundations in Professional Development** 20
Introduction 20
Foundations for Professional Learning 21
Site Selection 21
Learning From Others: Models and Menus 23
Laying the Footings: Deep, Wide, and Durable 24
Deep Enough 24
Wide Enough 27
Durable Enough 28
Laying Footings in Professional Development
That Are Deep, Wide, and Durable 29
Personal Actions 29
Creating Structures 30
Creating a Learning Culture 31
Developing Political Support 32
Defining Professional Development 32
Learning Opportunities 34
Engagement 35
Improved Practice 36
Conclusion 37

3. **Creating a Professional Learning Community** 40
Introduction 40
Professional Learning Community: What Is It? 41
Professional: More Than a License 42
Learning 44
Community 46
A Powerful Combination:
Professional-Learning-Community 47
Strategies for Building a Professional
Learning Community 48
Assessing Attributes of Professional
Learning Community 51
The Unlearning School Community 52
Conclusion 53

**PART II CREATING LEARNING SPACES
IN AND BEYOND WORK**   **57**

4. **Professional Development "As" Work**   **59**
    Introduction   59
    Expanding the Concept of Professional Development   60
        Rethinking Professional Development:
            New State Regulations   60
        Professional Development and Teacher Evaluation 61
    The Nature and Context of Professional Work in Schools 61
        Characteristics of Professional Work in Schools 62
    Toward a New Architecture for Professional
        Development: Three Major Shifts   66
        Conceptual Shifts   68
        Structural Shifts   68
        Cultural Shifts   70
    Implications for Educational Stakeholders   72
        Implications for Teachers   72
        Implications for Administrators   73
        Implications for School Boards   74
    Conclusion   74

5. **Professional Development "In" Work**   **77**
    Introduction   77
    Defining Professional Development "In" Work   78
    Job-Embedded Learning: Some Things We Know   79
    Advantages to Professional Development "In" Work   80
    Professional Learning "In" Work   81
        Individual Informal   82
        Individual Structured   83
        Collaborative Informal   83
        Collaborative Structured   84
    Limitations to Job-Embedded Learning   84
    Motivators and Barriers to Professional
        Development "In" Work   86
    Conclusion   88

6. **Professional Development "At" Work**   **92**
    Introduction   92
    Surveying the Landscape of Workplace Learning   93
        Workplace Learning in Schools   93
        A Cautionary Note on Workplace Learning in Schools 95

Professional Development "At" Work:
    A Familiar Paradigm   95
Creating Optimal Conditions for Workplace Learning   97
    Social Organization of School   97
    Resources   98
    Individual and Team Characteristics   101
Workplace Learning: Promises and Problems   101
Conclusion   102

7. Professional Development "Outside" of Work   106
Introduction   106
What is Professional Development "Outside" of Work?   107
Barriers to Professional Development "Outside" of Work   108
Creating and Supporting Professional
    Development "Outside" of Work   110
    Integrative/Connected Designs   112
    Delivery and Content   112
    Professional Development Context:
        Support for Professional Learning "Outside" of Work   113
    Professional Development Outcomes   114
Sharing Professional Knowledge: Team Learning   115
    Team Learning in Action: Three Vignettes   117
Conclusion   118

8. Professional Development "Beyond" Work   123
Introduction   123
Broadening and Deepening Our Understanding
    of Professional Development   124
Beyond Technique   126
Professional Development Journeys "Beyond" Work   127
    Journeying Out There   128
    The Journey Inward   130
Conclusion   133

**PART III   EVALUATING AND IMPLEMENTING NEW
DESIGNS FOR PROFESSIONAL LEARNING   137**

9. Evaluating the Architecture of Professional Development   139
Introduction   139
Utilitas, Firmitas, and Venustas: A Reprise   140
Why Evaluate Professional Development?   142
Evaluating Professional Development:
    Purposes and Contexts   143
Critical Levels of Professional Development Evaluation   144

Participants' Reactions: Journey to a Sami Camp 145
Participants' Learning: Classroom Action Research 146
Organizational Support and Change: Peer Coaching 147
Participants' Use of New Knowledge and Skills: Off-Site
    Technology Training 148
Student Learning Outcomes: Teacher Study Groups 148
Constructing Successful Professional
    Development Evaluations 149
Conclusion 151

10. From Design Studio to School Site   **153**
Introduction 153
Reviewing the Landscape of Professional Development 154
    Breaking the Box 154
    Building Beneath the Surface: Footings and
        Foundations in Professional Development 154
    Creating a Professional Learning Community 155
    Professional Development "As" Work 155
    Professional Development "In" Work 155
    Professional Development "At" Work 156
    Professional Development "Outside" of Work 156
    Professional Development "Beyond" Work 157
    Evaluating the Architecture of
        Professional Development 157
Confronting Challenges in Designs
    for Professional Learning 157
The Language of Architecture 159
    Professional Development Is About Learning 159
    Professional Development Is Work 160
    Professional Expertise Is a Journey, Not a Credential 160
    Opportunities for Professional Learning Are Unbounded 161
    Student Learning, Professional Development, and
        Organizational Mission Are Intimately Related 161
    Professional Development Is About People,
        Not Programs and Activities 162

Index   **163**

List of Tables and Figures

List of Tables

Table 2.1. Site Survey: Assessing Levels of Action 33

Table 3.1. Learning Principles: Implications
for Professional Development in Practice 45

Table 5.1. Professional Learning "In" Work:
Motivators and Barriers 87

Table 6.1. A Synthesis of Research on
Workplace Learning 94

Table 6.2. Professional Development "At" Work 96

Table 7.1. Professional Development "Outside" of Work 107

Table 7.2. Common Barriers and Limitations
to Professional Development "Outside" of Work 109

Table 7.3. Characteristics of Successful Professional
Development 111

List of Figures

Figure 1.1. The Architecture of Professional
Development: Essential Components 6

Figure 2.1. Site Survey: Commitment to
Professional Learning 26

Figure 2.2. Laying the Foundation: Four Levels of Action 29

Figure 2.3. Defining Professional Development 34

Figure 3.1. Professional Learning Community 43

Figure 3.2. Elements of Responsive Community 47

Figure 3.3. Two Contrasting Images of
Professional Learning Community 49

Figure 4.1. Toward a New Architecture for Professional
Development: Conceptual Shifts 67

Figure 4.2. Toward a New Architecture for
    Professional Development: Structural Shifts   69
Figure 4.3. Toward a New Architecture for
    Professional Development: Cultural Shifts   71
Figure 5.1. Professional Development "In" Work   81
Figure 6.1. Common Workplace Elements in
    Learning Enriched Schools   98
Figure 6.2. Creating Time for Professional Development   100
Figure 9.1. Critical Levels of Professional Development
    Evaluation   146
Figure 9.2. Key Elements for Successful Evaluation of
    Professional Development   150

Preface

There is something about a construction site that fascinates me. From my 12th floor office, I enjoy watching new shapes and structures across campus emerging from the ground. By any measure, each of these projects is evidence of a dynamic university that celebrates and extends the boundaries of teaching, learning, and research. Each new facility adds to the physical infrastructure that supports the multiple missions of our university community well into the next century. But something is missing, and I begin to wonder about connections between designs for buildings and designs for learning. While we spend enormous sums on physical structures, how much do we invest in reflecting on creating teaching and learning spaces within these buildings. More specifically, what pedagogical infrastructures are we designing to support faculty learning that enhances student learning? Is there a planning commission for faculty professional development? Creating physical space is the work of architects and contractors; teachers create optimal spaces for teaching and learning in their work. As a teacher and an architect, my campus walks and my professional journey bring me to a place where I propose *A New Architecture for Professional Development*.

Because professional development is closely linked with school improvement and student learning, strengthening professional development needs to be at the center of educational reform in the United States and around the world. Not least because it is difficult to find educational reform reports that do not include professional development as a component of school improvement. The good news is that, unlike many areas of education, the need for high-quality professional development is not part of education's disputed terrain. Teachers and their unions, administrators, board members, policy makers, and other community members understand the need for ongoing professional learning that strengthens professional practice and supports educational reform and school improvement focused on student learning. Within this context, there is a compelling need for professional learning, both individual and collective, to be legitimized as professional work and embedded in the daily work of teachers and administrators. Professional development is "time on," not "time off."

The new architecture for professional development is anchored in six design principles.

- Professional development is about learning.
- Professional development is work.
- Professional expertise is a journey, not a credential.
- Opportunities for professional learning and improved practice are unbounded.
- Student learning, professional development, and organizational mission are intimately related.
- Professional development is about people, not programs.

The purpose of this book is to propose a set of design principles for expanding and legitimizing learning opportunities for teachers and other professional educators in schools. Using the metaphor of architecture, the book proposes new designs for creating learning spaces for professional educators that challenge the boundaries, forms, and purposes of traditional design, delivery, content, and outcomes of professional development. Building on empirical research and exemplary practices, the book provides examples of professional learning expressed in this new architecture in its most natural setting—in schools and classrooms. Formal and informal professional learning beyond the school are also included in the landscape for professional learning.

My hope is that by using the metaphor of architecture for professional development, this book will be as intellectually evocative as it is practically grounded. The new architecture for professional development is helpful as a guide to educators, individually and collectively, as they think about, plan, and engage in professional learning and growth. New designs for professional learning spaces in and beyond schools provide a highly accessible framework for planning, carrying out, and assessing the impact of professional development in schools. The new architecture for professional development is nested in the landscape of real schools with real people, in real communities. New designs for professional learning are not isolated sketches in design studio portfolios. They are dynamic, oftentimes organic, creations built in communities of professional practice. Through careful descriptions of exemplary practices, I attempt to provide both an evocative intellectual and practical catalyst that stimulates educators' thinking, promotes professional learning and growth, and enhances practice. The proposed new architecture requires three fundamental shifts in the landscape of professional development—rethinking, restructuring, and reculturing to create professional learning communities that expand the horizons for professional learning beyond models and activities. The text's architecture also invites the reader to interact with new ideas, dimensions, and designs for professional learning. Internet sites and hot links to research, exemplary practices in schools, educator networks, and assessment tools are provided for immediate access and use by preK–12 teachers and administrators, education specialists, staff development personnel, educational trainers, higher education personnel, and consultants.

Because there have been significant changes in educator certification and licensing standards across the nation, I believe this book also provides a timely and helpful framework for addressing both practical and policy issues related to new educator licensing regulations and career advancement. The design principles in the new architecture provide guidelines for understanding and designing opportunities for professional learning that promote individual growth and improved professional practice, meet school improvement and educational reform goals, and support new licensing regulations, all of which ultimately better serve students.

You might ask: *What is new here*? *Do we really need another book on professional development*? Let me offer my response. To begin, the reader will find much that is familiar in the elements of architecture for professional development proposed here. But as architects design structures that make use of common elements (concrete, wood, and glass) often in unique and creative ways, architects for professional learning use familiar elements (workshops, study groups, and collaborative networks) to create artful designs with structural integrity appropriate to teachers' and administrators' needs. As such, the new architecture for professional development is not about creating the one, best model. The illusion of getting it right and establishing the best professional development practice does not fit the realities of schools nor the complexities of who teachers and administrators are and what they do. The new architecture for professional development is an ongoing creative process that brings new designs, interprets new realities, and at times, helps us rediscover those essential features that touch the minds, hearts, and souls of educators.

AUDIENCE

This book is intended for educational professionals who work daily to create learning spaces for students and themselves. Teachers, principals, curriculum and staff development specialists, superintendents, and professional association personnel will find this book anchored in the realities of their work lives in schools. Educational consultants, especially training and development personnel, will find this book helpful as they design learning opportunities for professionals in schools and in many other types of organizations. Though the book focuses on professional learning in schools, the design themes, exemplary practices, frameworks, and tools for designing, implementing, and assessing professional development are grounded in principles of adult learning and human cognition that underpin professional learning and growth in all organizations.

This book is also intended for the broader audience of local, state, and national policy makers. The designs for professional learning described in the book provide useful frameworks, examples in practice, and assessment tools that will inform policies that nurture and support the creation of learning enriched environments in schools for students and staff.

At the university level, professors of teacher education, educational leadership and policy studies, adult education, and continuing education will use this as a primary text for courses in the area of professional development and as a supplementary guide for training and staff development program planning and for designing innovations in professional development practices in organizations.

SUMMARY OF CHAPTERS

In the first chapter, "Breaking the Box: New Designs for Professional Learning in Schools," I use the metaphor of architecture to propose that we need to break the mold of traditional staff development and training by rethinking, restructuring, and reculturing schools and communities for professional learning. I introduce a set of design principles for creating a new architecture for professional development that reconsiders the design, delivery, content, context, and outcomes of professional learning. In "Building Beneath the Surface: Footings and Foundations in Professional Development," Chapter 2, I define professional development and describe how to prepare the site and lay the foundations for new designs for professional learning. Foundations must be wide enough, deep enough, and durable enough to provide the support—personal, structural, political, and cultural—on which new structures for professional learning are built. Chapter 3, "Creating a Professional Learning Community," examines the essential elements used to build professional learning communities. The chapter ends with a discussion of how authentic professional learning communities deal with the persistent paradox of learning and unlearning by developing individual and collective capacities to systematically unlearn (abandon) unproductive or outmoded structures, processes, practices, and ways of thinking. In the next five chapters of the book, I present rich illustrations of professional learning that express the designs features of the new architecture for professional development. In Chapter 4, "Professional Development 'As' Work," I go beyond traditional views of professional learning and practice by arguing that professional development is not something in addition to work, it is an essential part of educators' professional work. In "Professional Development 'In' Work," Chapter 5, I describe how professional learning is inextricably embedded in teachers' and administrators' daily work. While carrying out their primary work, educators can tap into continuous opportunities to gain new knowledge, practice and refine skills, reflect on individual and collective experiences, and deepen insights on teaching and learning. Chapter 6, "Professional Development 'At' Work," describes on-site workplace professional learning including in-service training, workshops, meetings, and school exchanges as another dimension of the new architecture for professional development. I explore the important advantages of "at" work learning as well as some potential negatives effects. I make the case that professional learning communities find ways to create optimal conditions that support professional development "at" work while mitigating any potential negative learning outcomes. Off-site professional learning is the focus of Chapter 7, "Professional Development 'Outside' of Work." After a discussion of the wide variety of professional learning opportunities away from school, I describe how successful learning communities build collective professional capacity by developing strategies to share new knowledge, skills, and wisdom from off-site, oftentimes individual learning experiences. In Chapter 8, "Professional Development 'Beyond' Work," I examine the terrain of various enriching life experiences and learning opportunities away from work and school that have the potential to enhance professional practice. I describe two types of professional development journeys beyond work. The first is a journey *out there* far beyond schools and work. The second is an inward journey connecting work, life, and learning. Both take teachers and administrators well beyond daily routines to vistas that give them new insights and deeper understandings of themselves, their work, and the world in which they live. "Evaluating the Architecture of Professional Development," Chapter 9, focuses on the assessment of the new architecture for professional development. I use several frameworks to illustrate ways to evaluate four key evaluation concerns—purpose, value, methods, and utility. The chapter also provides a framework of essential components for building credible and useful evaluations of new designs for professional learning. In Chapter 10, "From Design Studio to School Site," I review the landscape of professional development and describe challenges that confront policy makers and practitioners as they rethink, restructure, and reculture the architecture for professional development in their schools and communities. Using the six design themes as a reprise, the chapter closes with a discussion of the messages and meaning communicated in the new architecture for professional development.

ACKNOWLEDGMENTS

Completing a book project is both an exhilarating and a humbling experience. It is exciting to see the book I had once only vaguely imagined take shape after two years of reflection and writing. At the same time it is a humbling experience to know that this work represents only a small part of a much larger mosaic of professional practice and scholarship in the area of professional development. I am indebted to all of those authors, researchers, staff development personnel, teachers, and school administrators whose work, whether in print or in practice, have contributed immensely to my thinking and writing. As with any project, there are some people who deserve special thanks for their support. I am grateful to Corwin Press and to Rachel Livsey for her enthusiasm and encouragement in writing this book. I am truly thankful for professional colleagues at the University of Wisconsin-Madison and others around the world whose work and ideas have stimulated and enriched my own work. I am especially indebted to Olof Johansson for his generous invitation to spend a significant part of my sabbatical leave at Umea University in northern Sweden where I wrote the prospectus for this book. I also want to acknowledge the special contributions to form and content made by Eric J. Anctil. His background and resource work, as well as his editing suggestions, were invaluable contributions to this book. I also want to thank Maureen Adams and Van Lori Himbergen for sharing their work in this book. Though they remain unknown, I am deeply appreciative to three external reviewers, all of whom are practicing professionals, whose thoughtful and constructive reviews of the initial draft of this book helped me sharpen some of the arguments, enhance the overall presentation, and illustrate keys points with examples in practice. Finally, I want to thank my wife, Mary C. Bredeson, a Learning Resource Coordinator in Verona Area School District, Verona, Wisconsin, for sharing her own commitment to professional learning and for being a daily reminder to me that the new architecture for professional development is about people who dedicate their lives to the challenges and joys of learning in schools.

The contributions of the following reviewers are gratefully acknowledged:

Susan Mundry
Project Director
WestEd
Stoneham, MA

Laura Crehan
Educational Consultant
San Diego, CA

William A. Sommers
Executive Director
Minneapolis Public Schools
Minneapolis, MN

Elizabeth Lolli
Director of Curriculum
Mayfield City Schools
Highland Heights, OH

Lorraine M. Zinn
Owner and Senior Consultant
Lifelong Learning Options
Boulder, CO

Jacqueline LaRose
Staff Developer
Guilderland Central School District
Guilderland, NY

About the Author

Paul V. Bredeson is a Professor of Educational Administration at the University of Wisconsin-Madison where he teaches courses in Professional Development and Organizational Learning, Instructional Leadership and School Improvement, and Research Methods. He has been a Professor at Ohio University and at Pennsylvania State University where he also served as the Executive Director of the Pennsylvania School Study Council. Before entering higher education, he was a High School Principal and Spanish Teacher in Wisconsin and Connecticut respectively.

During the past 20 years, his research has centered on alternative conceptions of leadership and professional learning in schools. Grounded in his professional work experiences, his research and writing has two major strands. The first strand centers on the intersection of professional work and learning. The second focuses on the impact of alternative conceptualizations of leadership on the work of school principals.

Part I

Redesigning Professional Learning for Educators

1

Breaking the Box: New Designs for Professional Learning in Schools

Every piece of architecture has to be secured in a landscape. Especially if there is a new direction–there must be a landscape strategy that positions it.[1]

INTRODUCTION

At the beginning of the twentieth century, Frank Lloyd Wright, an aspiring young architect, rejected the formality and dominant design principles of American architecture. During the next 60 years, his prairie school designs harmonizing space, landscape, and people's lives transformed 20th century architecture. Many of his buildings, including the Guggenheim, Taliesin, and Fallingwater are among the most recognizable structures in the world.[2]

However, his most profound impact was on a more familiar structure, the typical American home. Close your eyes for a moment and imagine a 19th century Victorian home. Perhaps you see a tall, two-story house with a steep roof, sharply pointed gables, and a turret. The house's imposing size and height are

Site Visits

www.taliesinpreser-
vation.org; www.
wpconline.org/
fallingwaterhome.htm

3

squeezed on to a small city lot resembling a middle-aged man forced into tight blue jeans—spilling over the edges. Victorian rectitude is emphasized by the structure's crisp lines and symmetry in tall rectangular windows. In a few cases, however, 19th century uprightness gives way to gingerbread gables and garish colors, the neighborhood's painted ladies.

Now let us look at this structure through Wright's eyes and imagination. First, he believed this house at the turn of the last century reflected more the formality of Victorian architecture than it did the realities of how people actually lived. He forcefully argued that the Victorian house, "lied about everything. It had no sense of unity at all nor any such sense of space as should belong to a free people. . . . It began somewhere way down in the wet and ended as high up as it could get in the high and narrow. . . . This 'house' was a bedeviled box with a fussy lid; a complex box that had to be cut up by all kinds of holes made in it to let in light and air, with an especially ugly hole to go in and come out of."[3] He chafed at the boxlike rooms that confined interior space, walled out the natural environment, and limited the flow of movement and daily living.

When I first read this description, I was struck by how accurately it described the "bedeviled box" of teacher professional development at the beginning of a new century. Like the Victorian house a hundred years earlier, the major design features of contemporary teacher professional development reflect a legacy of teacher isolation, norms of privacy, fragmentation, and incoherence with far too little attention paid to the current realities of teachers' work and daily lives in schools. Though I have no illusions about comparing myself with America's most famous architect, I would argue that teacher professional development needs a similar transformation that asks teachers to think about their learning and its connections to their primary work, teaching children. This book is about a new architecture for creating learning spaces that provide teachers and administrators opportunities to learn, grow, and improve their professional practice.

The purpose of this book is to propose a set of design principles for expanding and legitimizing learning opportunities for teachers and other professional educators in and beyond schools. Using the metaphor of architecture, the book proposes new designs for creating learning spaces for professional educators that challenge the boundaries, forms, and purposes of traditional design, delivery, content, and outcomes of professional development. Building on empirical research and exemplary practices, the book provides examples of professional learning expressed in this new architecture in its most natural setting—in schools and classrooms. Formal and informal professional learning beyond the school are also included in the landscape of professional learning. Like Wright's prairie style homes featuring natural materials and using the natural contours of surrounding landscapes, I believe the new architecture for professional development must similarly use familiar materials and shapes that fit naturally into the landscape of teachers' and administrators' daily work.

THINKING OUTSIDE AND BEYOND THE BOX

When confronted with seemingly intractable problems, we often ask people to think outside of the box—beyond familiar structures, common solutions, and generally accepted notions of what is possible and what is not. Novel ideas and unforeseen possibilities often emerge from such an activity. Any new ideas, however, will be put back into the original box with some modest adjustments. Another way of thinking about this generative process is simply to do away with the box and its inherent limitations. The novel ideas then become catalysts for transformation. Like the reconceptualized spaces in Wright's creations, I invite you to think beyond the traditional box of staff development and to consider radically transforming professional learning spaces for teachers and administrators. My hope is that this book will engage you in ways that help you think about professional development in new ways, not simply ones that fit familiar teacher routines and current school structures. The new architecture breaks the professional development box by challenging the traditional design, delivery, content, context, and outcomes of teacher professional development.

UTILITAS, FIRMITAS, AND VENUSTAS: ESSENTIAL COMPONENTS OF ARCHITECTURE

In one of the most readable books on architecture that I have encountered, *ABC of Architecture*, James O'Gorman[4] cites the classic work of an ancient Roman architect and engineer, Vitruvius, whom he credits for the most succinct and encompassing definition of architecture ever written. Vitruvius's definition describes three essential components of architecture—function (utilitas), structure (firmitas), and beauty (venustas). In Figure 1.1 the three components are displayed as corners of an equilateral triangle. "Each is discrete, yet all combine to shape a larger whole."[5] Professional development is a human endeavor, like architecture, that brings the three components together. Let us look more closely at how these components are expressed in the architecture of professional development.

Function (Utilitas)

The first corner of the triangle represents the function of professional development. One of the major responsibilities of any architect is to listen and respond to the needs, interests, and priorities of clients. In the area of professional development, this means that the design, delivery, and intended outcomes of learning activities are to serve the interest of clients. Who are the clients of professional development? Whose interests are being served? Who benefits from professional development in schools?

Figure 1.1   The Architecture of Professional Development: Essential Components

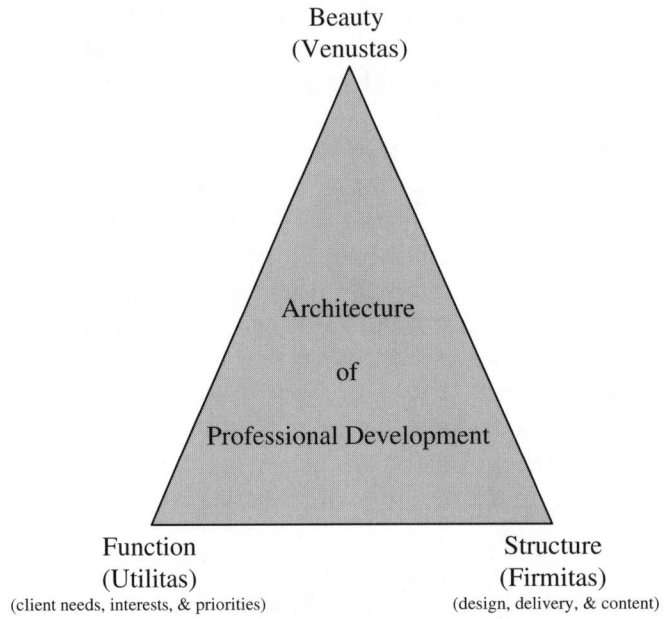

The most obvious clients of professional development are teachers and principals. After all, they are the participants in the learning activities. Various professional development programs and strategies are designed to meet educators' needs, helping them learn and grow as people and professionals with the expressed intention of strengthening their professional practice and its outcomes. Though teachers and administrators are the major participants, they are not the only beneficiaries (clients). Professional development is also intended to improve student learning outcomes, improve the quality of educators' work life, facilitate organizational change, support local school improvement efforts as well as broader educational reform, contribute to community building, and last, enhance the quality and impact of the professions of teaching and administration. When we consider the function of professional development in schools, serving client interests includes a wide range of activities with multiple beneficiaries.

Structure (Firmitas)

The second corner of the architecture of professional development triangle is structure. In the area of professional development, structure refers to the structural and material components that are brought together to meet the needs of clients. This includes the elements of design, delivery, and content of learning opportunities. Structures are the concrete and visible dimensions of professional development experiences that we create to address the interests of teachers, administrators, and schools, including learning experiences "in," "at," "outside," and "beyond" work, as well as the organizational processes and systems that support them.

The relationship of interdependence between professional development structures and function is obvious, but nonetheless, often ignored. For instance, planning and implementing staff development activities may be more the result of convenience and organizational expediency than based on the critical needs and interests of staff. When professional development structures emerge without clear purpose and priorities that meet the needs and interests of teachers and administrators, the result is fragmented and faddish activities masquerading as professional learning. Consequently, there is little wonder why many educators remain wary, cynical, and frustrated by traditional inservice and staff development activities that are designed and implemented without their input.

Beauty (Venustas)

The third corner of the architecture of professional development triangle is beauty. When I first began to reflect on this essential element in architecture, I thought about the common admonition: beware of making arguments that rely on metaphors. Up to this point, the metaphor of architecture has been a friendly linguistic, conceptual companion that has helped me make my case for rethinking and recreating professional development in education. After all, metaphors are powerful cognitive and linguistics devices. Still, we are reminded that metaphors are suggestive comparisons, not exact copies. I believe we need to consider the notion of aesthetics in professional development further.

The element of beauty seems so apparent in such architectural wonders as the Taj Mahal, Taliesin, the Sydney Opera House, and the Alhambra.[6] Yet, it seems less obvious in the context of professional learning. I have some questions regarding the applicability of beauty to the architecture of professional development:

- What are the aesthetic elements in the architecture of professional development?
- Is beauty in the architecture of professional development solely in the "eye of the beholder"?
- If beauty is an essential component in architecture, why has so little attention been given to aesthetics of professional development?

In professional development, beauty comes from the artistic arrangement and use of materials and systems to create learning spaces that engage teachers and administrators in learning opportunities that meet their needs and change them as people and professionals. "Beauty, architectural beauty, is the hoped-for result of appropriate planning and sturdy structure."[7]

Creating new designs for professional learning for educators is anchored in these same essential architectural components. The work of architects for professional development is to create artful designs for learning (venustas) with structural integrity (firmitas) that appropriately meet the needs of teachers, administrators, and the students and communities they serve (utilitas).

PROFESSIONAL DEVELOPMENT DESIGN THEMES

In a tour of Taliesin, home to Frank Lloyd Wright's design studio and prairie school of architecture in Spring Green, Wisconsin, tour guides often point out a small glass case. In it are children's blocks—geometric shapes—squares, rectangles, cylinders, and triangles—that Wright played with as a child. Were these blocks only artifacts from Wright's 19th century childhood, they would be interesting but hardly noteworthy. What makes them an important exhibit is their relationship to his work as an architect. These basic geometric shapes reappear in new and oftentimes unexpected ways in some of his most famous buildings. From child's play to creative genius, Wright relied on familiar, ordinary shapes. These shapes became design themes, and despite their ordinariness, his creativity transformed these shapes into distinctive signatures on such architectural masterpieces as the Guggenheim in New York City, Fallingwater in Mill Run, Pennsylvania, and the S.C. Johnson & Son Administration Building in Racine, Wisconsin. Like the geometric shapes in Wright's buildings, the new architecture for professional development in education has design themes that draw on familiar and ordinary features, but ones used in different and novel ways. There are six design themes in the new architecture for professional development.

Design Theme One
- Professional development is about learning.

Design Theme Two
- Professional development is work.

Design Theme Three
- Professional expertise is a journey not a credential.

Design Theme Four
- Opportunities for professional learning and improved practice are unbounded.

Design Theme Five
- Student learning, professional development, and organizational mission are intimately related.

Design Theme Six
- Professional development is about people, not programs.

Design Theme One—Professional Development Is About Learning

It is ironic that schools, ostensibly organized to nurture and support student intellectual, moral, and social development, are often sterile, at times even hostile, environments for professional learning. Interestingly, the things we know and practice related to children's learning and development are often missing when it comes to the design, delivery, and assessment of professional development in schools. Though learning can occur even under adverse conditions, we know from research and experience that individual learning is maximized when there is an optimal mix of instructional, curricular, developmental, and environmental factors organized in ways that stimulate and support the learner.

As a design theme, recognizing that professional development is about learning keeps the focus on the learner. Too often the emphasis in professional development is on the activity (a workshop, a speaker, or a conference) and not on the learner's needs. Keeping the focus on learning principles, let's draw on our wealth of professional knowledge about learning.

For example, we know that:

- Learners at different stages of development have different needs.
- Learners have different learning style preferences that affect their learning.
- Learners' prior knowledge greatly influences their learning.
- Learners' motivation and opportunities for reflection are critical to learning.

Now replace the word "learner" with teacher or with principal. Are these principles of learning evident in the design and delivery of professional learning in your school? In what ways do these fundamental understandings of human cognition influence how you think about professional development in your school? Of course, we know much more than these four bulleted items about human cognition. My point here is that we simply need to apply what we know about learning to professional development in schools. The principles are familiar ones. Using these fundamental principles of learning, we can configure new ways that support professional learning, growth, and improved practice—the essence of a professional learning community.

Design Theme Two—Professional Development Is Work

The fact that teachers and principals are learners and continue to be throughout their careers is not new. Highly skilled educators have long been involved in summer institutes, inservice training, graduate degree programs, and countless other formal and informal activities to gain new knowledge and skills to improve their practice. What is new is the increased emphasis being placed on professional development and its links to school improvement, organizational development, and enhanced student learning. Traditionally, professional development has been relegated to after-school meetings, summers, and off-work hours. Researchers, policy makers, and practitioners now recognize that professional development cannot be an add-on to the end of an already busy workday, nor can it be just an option for those who are interested. Opportunities to learn are not organizational frills and they should not be subjected to the whims of capricious budget cutting exercises. Ongoing professional learning must be a dimension of professional work embedded in daily routines and organizational culture.[8] For this to happen in schools, professional development must be seen as legitimate work, essential to professional expertise and exemplary practice. The challenge is to provide the structures, processes, and resources during educators' workdays so that they can learn and reflect on what they have learned in terms of their practice.

Design Theme Three—Professional Expertise Is a Journey Not a Credential

At one time in our educational history, teachers could simply complete their training programs, receive their licenses, and practice until they decided to move on or retire. There were few, if any, formal requirements beyond initial preservice preparation. Ease of entry, and minimal licensing requirements into teaching and school administration, suggested to some that education was a convenient fallback for employment if other opportunities did not work out. Like the one-room schoolhouse and filmstrip projector, those days are gone. Teaching and school leadership are complex, demanding jobs. Preservice training, clinical experiences, and probationary licenses are the beginning phases of the professional socialization journey in teaching and school leadership. In many states, new license requirements for teachers and principals recognize that beginning educators are novices and, therefore, need additional knowledge and skill development under structured and supportive environments before they can be granted advanced licenses to practice. During this probationary period, employing school districts and state licensing authorities require practitioners to design plans for professional growth and development with clear goals and documented evidence of professional competencies. License renewal also requires a plan for ongoing professional growth and development. The central message regarding the career licensing requirements for teachers and administrators is clear. This is a journey that requires commitment to high standards of practice and ongoing professional development.

Design Theme Four—Opportunities for
Professional Learning That Informs Practice Are Unbounded

Recently, I spent a day at a Sami (Laplander) camp in far northern Sweden. My hosts and I traveled miles by snowmobile to a remote winter camp where we lassoed reindeer, competed in sled races, and feasted on fire-roasted reindeer, bread, and strong coffee under a tent of deerskins. The day was full of adventure, new experiences, and vivid images. What I did not know at the time was the impact these experiences would have on my professional thinking and practice. No, I have not incorporated reindeer roasting or races into my teaching. In fact, it is likely my students are quite unaware of my experiences with the Sami. Nevertheless, I believe it was a transformative learning experience. I had been introduced to a unique culture with a worldview different from my own. My assumptions and understandings about life and professional work in the modern world had been challenged; the dissonance created a tension that stretched my thinking and my being.

As a design principle, lived experiences transformed into professional learning provide elements of surprise and serendipity that fire the mind, heart, and soul. Beyond the box of traditional professional development are limitless possibilities for enriching, energizing, and informing educators' professional thinking and work. This is not an argument for doing away with such formal learning as staff development, training, and other traditional forms of professional development. It is, however, one that nurtures and affirms learning opportunities in teachers' and principals' lives beyond classrooms and schools.

Design Theme Five—Student Learning, Professional
Development, and Organizational Mission Are Intimately Related

One of the unanticipated consequences of specialization in complex organizations such as schools is fragmentation and a sense of disconnection. Schools and the people in them are susceptible to silos of separation and specialization. Much of this is a legacy of the organizing principles of industrial America. During the 19th century, as public schools grew exponentially in numbers and with more diverse student populations, educational leaders and policy makers looked to other societal sectors—mining, railroads, manufacturing industries, and the military—for ideas to organize, administer, and operate schools.[9] The major organizing principles of industrial America—specialization, maximization, centralization, concentration, and standardization—became familiar ones to educators much the same as total quality management ideas are common in today's schools.[10] Schools had not always been organized around such principles. Educators purposely rethought the organization and operation of schools in new ways to meet new social and economic realities. Though it will not be easy, new realities and challenges again demand new ways of thinking about schools and the professionals who work in them. I believe this will be accomplished by rethinking schools and professional work in ways that link purpose, people, and possibilities for human growth and development into a new whole—a professional learning community. This means thinking in systemic, integrative ways. What is important is seeing the interdependence among student learning, professional development, and organizational purposes. There are, to be sure, important distinctions among these areas, but when combined, they have enormous organizational and human generative power and synergy.

Design Theme Six—Professional Development Is About People, Not Programs

The ancient Chinese statesperson, Guan Zhong, captured the essence of this design theme when he described the long view of development in his country: "The plan for a year is growing grains. The plan for a decade is planting trees. And, the plan for life is nurturing people." The new architecture of professional development is fundamentally about people and their essential humanity. While the technical, cultural, and structural dimensions of professional development are critical to success, the formation of educators' sense of identity and moral purpose is more than an accumulation of technical skills and professional competencies. As Parker Palmer reminds us, understanding the inner landscapes of teachers and discovering who they are as people and professionals are critical to supporting their development. "To chart that landscape fully, three important paths must be taken—intellectual, emotional, and spiritual—and none can be ignored. Reduce teaching to intellect, and it becomes a cold abstraction; reduce it to emotions, and it becomes narcissistic; reduce it to the spiritual, and it loses its anchor to the world. Intellect, emotion, and spirit depend on one another for wholeness."[11] Teachers and administrators also depend on one another for wholeness as they individually and collectively develop their capacities for learning and for strengthening their professional practice.

WHY IS IT IMPORTANT TO REDESIGN PROFESSIONAL DEVELOPMENT IN SCHOOLS?

There are at least five major reasons to redesign professional development in education.

Educator Work Is Complex and Demanding. The work of teachers and principals has become increasingly more complex and more demanding and requires greater expertise than at any time in the history of public education.

Consistent calls for teacher professional development is not an indictment of teacher professionalism, but rather recognition that the academic and social needs of today's children, especially those in impoverished rural and urban settings, require highly skilled teachers and principals with new knowledge, skills, and professional competencies. In 1940, for example, when teachers were asked to list major threats to their school community, they listed such transgressions as gum chewing, littering, breaking in line, violating dress codes, talking too loudly, and running in the halls. By the 1990s, teachers were confronted with new challenges including student suicide, assault, robbery, rape, premature pregnancy, and substance abuse.[12] Poverty, violence, child abuse and neglect, drugs, and homelessness are serious conditions that currently affect the nature of teachers' and principals' daily work. While student deportment remains an important issue, the severity of threat and the knowledge and skills teachers and principals need to deal effectively with students are dramatically different. Teaching has always been a demanding profession. However, the context of teachers' and principals' work today is clearly quite different from that found in 1940.

Workshops, guest speakers, various inservice meetings, and advanced degrees have been the primary ways educators have gained new knowledge to improve their practice. There is value to such activities. However, the fact that teachers and principals remain passive recipients and are provided only limited opportunities to reflect upon new information does little to provide them with the expert knowledge and skills to deal effectively with the range of problems and the educational needs of today's students. In addition to having command of their subject matter, teachers need to have a repertoire of teaching skills to work with students who may have multiple disabilities, be disaffected, or become violent. In addition, the infusion of new information technologies in schools compounds the need for increased emphasis on teacher learning and development. The nature and complexity of teaching requires more than a traditional "sit and get" inservice program carried out at the end of a school day.

Professional Development and School Improvement: An Emerging Consensus. A second major reason to redesign professional development is that reform reports and policy initiatives indicate that there is an emerging consensus that professional development is an important component of school improvement and educational reform more broadly. A review of policy and reform documents over the past decade indicates that one of the most powerful ways to enhance learning opportunities and outcomes for all children in public education is to improve the quality and expertise of teachers in our nation's classrooms. See, for example, Professional Development Guidelines, AFT, 1995; *Teaching as the Learning Profession: Handbook of Policy and Practice*, Darling-Hammond and Sykes, 1999; *What Matters Most: Teaching for America's Future*, NCTAF, 1996.[13] As documented

Site Visits

www.nsdc.org/library/
NSDCPlan.html;
www.npeat.org;
www.nfie.org/news.
htm

in the reports cited, the focus of school improvement initiatives and reform efforts is on higher student achievement.

Success in these areas is inextricably linked to the quality and accessibility of ongoing, learning opportunities for teachers and principals. Creating access and opportunity is the force shaping a new architecture for professional development in schools. Research and reports of exemplary practice suggest common characteristics of effective professional development for teachers and principals.

Effective professional development:

- Is continuous.
- Links student learning to educator needs and school goals.
- Is school-based and job-embedded.
- Is supported with resources—time, money, processes, and structures to ensure success.
- Integrates and focuses multiple innovations on student learning and success.
- Incorporates multiple data sources to plan, implement, and evaluate student learning and professional practices.
- Involves teachers and principals in the identification and design of learning experiences to meet individual and collective needs.

New Licensing Regulations. Recognizing the importance of professional development to school improvement and student achievement is necessary but not sufficient. A new architecture, one beyond the traditional professional development box, will create learning spaces that recognize the complexities and realities of teachers' and principals' work lives while simultaneously attending to their needs for ongoing growth and development that strengthen their practice. New designs for professional learning must also recognize the continuum of professional preparation and practice moving from novice to expert. Increasingly, state licensing boards are differentiating among professional licenses for educators by granting *probationary licenses* for beginning teachers and principals, *professional licenses* for career educators, and *advanced licenses* for candidates who demonstrate and document expert knowledge and competence. Professional development plans are important components of these licenses. Board certification by the National Board of Professional Teaching Standards, the National Association of School Psychologists, and the American Speech-Language-Hearing Association are examples of these types of professional credentials.[14]

The license renewal process for educators has undergone similar changes. Many states now require teachers and administrators to maintain and submit for license renewal a professional development plan that documents professional growth and its link to improved practice. Traditionally, teachers and administrators have completed certification programs in their specialties and then applied to the state for a license to practice. Typically, every five years they applied for a license renewal and paid the required fees. Though professional development has always been an implicit goal for career advancement and license renewal, today's licensing and renewal processes make professional development an explicit component of licensure.[15] No longer can teachers and administrators simply take six credits every five years, regardless of their connection to their work, and mail the documentation into the state for license renewal. Graduate credits at colleges and universities are important opportunities to gain professional knowledge and skills, but the case for relevance to one's practice and professional growth plans needs to be made. In addition, new licensing requirements legitimize a wide variety of professional development opportunities beyond traditional courses and graduate credits. These may include such activities as study groups, attendance at professional conferences as participants and presenters, action research projects, mentoring, and curriculum work teams.[16]

Accountability for Education Outcomes. A fundamental shift in the assessment of educational quality in the United States is also an important reason for redesigning professional development. Educational outcomes have always been important to teachers and principals. For many years, the way in which policy makers and practitioners traditionally examined educational quality was by evaluating the nature and quality of inputs into the educational system. This included such measures as the dollars spent per pupil, the breadth and depth of curricular offerings, the degree level and field of professional staff, physical space and equipment, and the ratio of staff to students. There is a large body of research that examines the link between the quality of inputs and educational outcomes.[17] Notwithstanding the importance of inputs to student success, the demand for greater accountability for student learning outcomes has become the new organizer for the assessment of educational quality. Responding to public demands and exercising political muscle, state legislatures across the nation, and more recently the federal government, mandated new standards holding districts, schools, administrators, and teachers accountable for "what students should know and be able to do," the new catch-phrase of the standards movement. Standards-based curricula, high stakes tests, and educational report cards are the new realities for the delivery and assessment of educational quality.

New regulatory requirements have intensified change initiatives across some 15,000 local school districts resulting in staff development and inservice training focusing their resources on compliance with new standards. Millions of dollars and countless hours invested by school districts are testament to the fundamental shift in the evaluation of educational quality centered on explicit student learning outcomes. Some educators remain skeptical arguing that the diversion of time, money, and energy centered on compliance with new state standards will have only limited impact on student learning outcomes. District and school compliance with standards is one thing; changing teachers' knowledge, beliefs, and instructional practices in classrooms is quite another.

Problems and Possibilities: Paradoxes in Professional Development. Despite the overwhelming consensus that professional development is critical to school improvement, there is an interesting paradox. On the one hand, there are numerous, perhaps inflated, promises from enthusiasts suggesting that professional development has remarkable restorative powers to revitalize teaching, improve instruction, transform schools, break the mold of traditional classroom practices, raise student achievement, address issues of inequality and racism, empower teachers, and redesign the curriculum and teachers' work. In contrast, there is a litany of problems that practitioners and scholars point out. The record indicates that staff development and inservice training in schools suffer from a number of limitations, including that they: (a) tend to be piecemeal, fragmented, and incoherent; (b) do little to change instructional practices; (c) generally are not integrated into teachers' daily work; (d) are too narrow in focus; (e) are poorly evaluated; (f) are not conceptually or programmatically linked to preservice teacher preparation; and (g) generally fail to provide adequate follow-up resources and support to sustain changes in teachers' practices and/or school structures. At this point you might want to throw up your hands in the proverbial gesture of "What's the use!" As Charles Handy reminds us, "Paradoxes are the like the weather, something to be lived with not solved, the worst mitigated, the best enjoyed and used as clues to the way forward."[18] My own sense of these contradictions is that they are the seedbed of tension that feeds creativity and forces us to find new ways to think about persistent problems and dilemmas surrounding educators' learning and professional practice. The contradictory streams of promises and problems provide an opportunity to rethink and redesign teacher and administrator learning in schools creating a new architecture for professional development in education.

CHANGING THE PARADIGM OF PROFESSIONAL DEVELOPMENT

At first, it is likely that some of the new designs for professional development in schools may look as strangely out of place as did some of Wright's prairie style homes set among 19th century traditional houses.

Redesigning professional development into a new architecture for career-long growth and development in schools will not be easy. Everyone is in favor of improvement in professional development; it is changing professional development as they know it that bothers them. Changing the paradigm requires rethinking, restructuring, and reculturing professional development.

Change in any complex system requires vision, requisite knowledge and skills, incentives, resources, and an action plan to bring it about.[19] Changing the paradigm of professional development requires a vision of where we want to be and what it should look like. Once we articulate a vision we can analyze the gap between where we are and where we want to be. Bridging the gap requires such things as new information, technologies, and skills. Because many people will be naturally hesitant about dramatic changes in professional development opportunities in schools, a set of incentives appropriate to the vision and to individual and organizational needs must be in place. This may include adjustments or alternatives to the current salary schedules driven by credits and years of experience. The new architecture for professional development in schools will require two major resources—time and money. External funds through grants, newly budgeted money, and reallocated dollars are primary financial resources. Redesigning time in ways that support the learning community for students and staff is also a critical resource. Finally, we need an action plan to move us successfully from where we are to where we want to be. The plan charts the course, coordinates the logistics, and evaluates progress toward our goal along the way. Each of these components will be is described in greater detail in subsequent chapters.

SITE VISITS

www.ncrel.org/pd/
The North Central Regional Educational Laboratory (NCREL) site highlights research and promising practices in professional development.
www.ed.gov/inits/teachers/eisenhower/
On-line version of Designing Effective Professional Development: Lessons from the Eisenhower Program.
www.nrpdc.org:8080/nrpdc/
The Northeast Regional Professional Development Center (Region 8) is one of 12 centers across Ohio organized to provide long-term, ongoing, and meaningful professional development for all K-12 educators.
www.ascd.org/
The Association for Supervision and Curriculum Development Web site features calendars of activities and resources for professional development.
www.nsdc.org/
The National Staff Development Council Web site offers listings of professional development activities, resources, and current activities.

SUPPLEMENTARY READINGS

Corcoran, T. C. (1995). *Transforming professional development for teachers: A guide for state policymakers*. Washington, DC: National Governors Association.

Guskey, T. R., & Huberman, M. (1995). *Professional development in education: New paradigms and practices*. New York: Teachers College Press.

Hassel, E. (1999). *Professional development: Learning from the best*. Oak Brook, IL: North Central Regional Educational Laboratory.

National Foundation for Improvement in Education. (1996). *Teachers take charge of their learning*. Washington, DC: Author.

National Staff Development Council. (1995). *Standards for staff development: (Elementary School; Middle School; and High School Editions)*. Oxford, OH: Author.

Sparks, D., & Hirsch, S. (1997). *A new vision for staff development*. Reston, VA: Association for Supervision and Curriculum Development.

U.S. Department of Education. (1999). *Designing effective professional development: Lessons from the Eisenhower Program*. Washington, DC: Author.

NOTES

1. Shepheard, P. (1995*). What is architecture? An essay on landscapes, buildings, and machines*. Cambridge, MA: MIT Press.

2. Retrieved July 1, 2000, from www.taliesinpreservation.org and www.wpconline.org/fallingwaterhome.htm

3. *Truth against the world: Frank Lloyd Wright speaks for an organic architecture*. Washington, DC: Preservation Press, National Trust for Historic Preservation.

4. O'Gorman, J. F. (1998). *ABC of architecture*. Philadelphia: University of Pennsylvania Press, 16.

5. Ibid., 12.

6. Retrieved July 1, 2000, from www.rubens.anu.edu.au/studentprojects/tajmahal/actualtomb.html for Taj Mahal; www.taliesinpreservation.org for Taliesin; www.soh.nsw.gov.au/virtual_tour/vrtour.html for Sydney Opera House; www.red2000.com/spain/granada/1photo.html for Alhambra.

7. O'Gorman., 4

8. Bredeson, P. V. (2000). Teacher learning as work and at work: Exploring the content and context of teacher professional development. *Journal of In-Service Education, 26*(1), 63–72.

9. Bredeson, P. V. (1988). Perspectives on schools: Metaphors and management in education. *Journal of Educational Administration, 29*(3), 293–310.

10. Toffler, A. (1970). *Future shock*. New York: Bantam Books.

11. Palmer, P. (1998). *The courage to teach: Exploring the inner landscape of a teacher's life*. San Francisco: Jossey-Bass, 4.

12. Glazer, S. (1992, September 11). Can anything be done to curb the growing violence? *Congressional Quarterly Researcher*. Retrieved July 1, 2002, from http://library.cqlibrary.com [1992, September 11]

13. See the following resources. Darling-Hammond, L., & Sykes, G. (1999). *Teaching as the learning profession: Handbook of policy and practice*. San Francisco: Jossey-Bass. NCTAF (1996). *What matters most: Teaching for America's future*. New York: National Commission on Teaching and America's Future. *Principles for professional development: AFT guidelines for creating professional development programs that make a difference Retrieved* July 1, 2002, from www.aft.org/edissues/downloads/ppd.pdf

14. Retrieved July 1, 2002, from www.nbpts.org; www.nasponline.org/index2.html; and www.asha.org

15. Retrieved July 1, 2002, from www.dpi.wi.us

16. Wisconsin Department of Public Instruction PI 34 regulations for licensure.

17. An excellent review of current research can be found in: Monk, D. H., & Plecki, M. L. (1999). *Generating and managing resources of school improvement*. In J. Murphy & K. Seashore Louis (Eds.), *Handbook of research on educational administration*. San Francisco: Jossey-Bass.

18. Handy, C. (1994). *The age of paradox*. Boston: Harvard Business School Press.

19. See "Factors in managing complex change" Knoster (1991) and Ambrose (1987). Retrieved July 1, 2002, from www.ctassets.org/pdf/reading/factorsmngng.pdf

2

Building Beneath the Surface: Footings and Foundations in Professional Development

If you have built castles in the air, your work need not be lost; that is where they should be. Now put foundations under them.[1]

INTRODUCTION

During the early 1970s, as many of our contemporaries did, my wife and I moved to the country, purchased 40 acres, and set about building a new life. Little did we realize at the time that the lessons learned building a cabin to live in, a barn, and a chicken house would provide the critical experiences and essential knowledge for understanding the foundations for professional development. Among the lessons about building that we learned early on was the need for careful planning, the appropriate tools matched to the job, and a solid base for construction. Each of these lessons has implications for building foundations to support professional learning in schools. The chapter begins with a discussion of the important work of building beneath the surface. I then describe three essential features for constructing footings that support new architectural designs for professional development. I argue that footings must be (a) deep enough, (b) wide enough, and (c) durable enough to give stability to professional development structures and their outcomes over time. In the final section, I define professional development.

FOUNDATIONS FOR PROFESSIONAL LEARNING

Footings are an invisible, yet essential, part of any building. The weight and forces above ground require the architect to find ways for the foundation to bear the load and balance competing pressures to provide support, stability, and integrity to the building. Architectural plans must consider the site on which the structure will be built; the surface and landscape features; the substrate beneath the surface; and the unique environmental and climatic conditions. Each of these influences the choices and decisions about the design and materials of the building's foundation. Like physical structures, professional development also relies on footings and foundations for support and stability. What do the footings and foundations for professional development look like in schools?

Site Selection

The unique features of a building site present architects with opportunities and constraints as they consider their designs. Similarly, unique school and community characteristics challenge professional development designers as they design learning opportunities appropriate to educators' needs and local context. Though there are many organizational and cultural similarities, no school or faculty is identical to another. The mix of history, culture, students, staff, goals, community setting, and resources dramatically affects the nature of individual schools. Even though we recognize unique school site characteristics, many traditional models of professional development fail to provide appropriate foundations for the school site and local conditions. The mismatch between well-intentioned learning activities and local context is at the heart of the vignette that follows.

> Early in my career as a school principal, I was enrolled in a graduate class in curriculum planning. One group from the class was assigned the task of developing innovative strategies for enriching a physical education curriculum. Using a "model" for curriculum planning, they presented a comprehensive design for activities that would meet learning objectives as well as provide unique and enriching experiences for students. One of the activities for curriculum enrichment included bringing the local dance troupe into schools to work with students. As I sat listening to this animated and highly engaging presentation, I thought about my school located in a very small town with one combination feed mill-grocery-hardware store, one bank, one gas station, and the local tavern. I considered what it would mean to invite the local dance troupe into my school. My mind raced wildly, then mischievously! The only dancer I could think of was Tullie, a rather colorful, and might I add exotic, patron of the tavern. When I taught in suburban Connecticut, I might have thought differently about the possibilities of a local dance troupe. Understanding local context, its possibilities and limitations, is critical as we assess sites and possibilities for professional development. Good ideas and best practices in some locations do not always fit the uniqueness of some school sites.

Educators frequently borrow concepts and ideas from other sectors—business, industry, and even the military. The language we use in schools, oftentimes with little thought of its original source, illustrates this point. We commonly hear such terms as *targets*, *strategic planning*, *total quality*, *zero defects*, *line and staff*, and *pay for performance*. More recently, we hear policy makers call for "taking various educational reform models to scale." Borrowing a concept from the manufacturing sector, well-intentioned reformers are buying into the notion that once a prototype has been developed and refined, it can be replicated across 15,000 school districts with little regard for unique local conditions and features.

Rather than designing the one best professional development practice, there is an emerging consensus in the literature suggesting a set of organizing principles and processes that teachers, administrators, and policy makers can use to design their own models for professional learning. For example, the North Central Regional Education Laboratory (NCREL) provides one such guidebook—a toolkit for designing effective and sustainable and professional development. Based on the experiences of national professional development award winners, the guidebook presents ideas and lessons for teachers, administrators, and policy makers to tailor professional development to the unique vision, goals, students, and professional staffs of local schools.[2]

Site Visit

www.ncrel.org

Professional Development: Learning From the Best. The one-size-fits-all inservice program all too common in education is perhaps the most blatant example of a prepackaged professional development activity imposed on a site with no regard for its unique characteristics or client needs. Because this form of staff development is so familiar to us, we often do not even think about how ill-suited it is to teachers' and principals' professional needs. To make my point, think about how difficult it would be for an architect to design a building with no information about the site on which it would be built. It would be difficult for an architect to design any structure in a vacuum—with no reference to site elevation, landscape, or use. Like the vignette above, think about the likely mismatches between structure and site. Imagine, for instance, Frank Lloyd Wright's Fallingwater, on the plains of Nebraska, or in an urban landscape. It seems ludicrous yet it happens all the time in schools. New programs are adopted, training is provided, and many educators stand back passively in awe of the strange designs in front of them wondering what these activities and plans have to do with their most critical professional needs.

Site Visit

www.wpconline.org/
fallingwaterhome.htm

Learning From Others: Models and Menus

There is much to learn from the experiences and designs others have developed to enhance professional learning and practice in local school districts. Making contributions to the field of education by sharing expertise, craft wisdom, and critical insights is one of the hallmarks of professionalism. There are common principles for effective models for professional learning.[3] Learning from colleagues is a major source of professional development for novices and for career educators. Nonetheless, we know that the ways in which individual educators develop their unique expertise are rarely identical to those of their professional peers. Thus, the idea of simply replicating various staff development models (best practices), without recognizing the unique features and characteristics of individuals and their work settings, wastes resources and feeds frustration on the part of teachers and principals. What do we need to know about the surface features, substrates, and environmental conditions that affect how we lay the foundation for professional learning for teachers and principals?

Site Visits

www.nsdc.org for
Standards for
Professional
Development;
www.ed.gov/inits/
teachers/eisenhower/
for Designing Effective
Professional
Development: Lessons
from the Eisenhower
Program

LAYING THE FOOTINGS:
DEEP, WIDE, AND DURABLE

In any school, the overall structure for professional learning and development for teachers and principals rests on footings that provide support and stability over time. I believe these footings require three essential features. They must be *deep enough* to withstand upheavals caused by severe conditions affecting the site. They must be *wide enough* to distribute the weight of the structures and processes to provide stability to professional learning. Finally, they must be *durable enough* so that over time they continue to provide the support needed to sustain professional development structures and their intended outcomes.

Deep Enough

The professional learning of teachers and principals is continually buffeted by changes in the political climate, budget vagaries, unforeseen social upheavals, and new work demands. To withstand various forces that may threaten the quality and environment for professional learning in schools, professional development must rest on deeply embedded values, commitment, and a clear sense of moral purpose. First and foremost, professional learning must be a deep, core value in the school community. Teachers, administrators, school board officials, and community members need to understand the value of continuous learning to high-quality professional practice that serves the needs of children in the district.

Valuing learning influences all aspects of the school. For instance, when learning is deeply valued, it is unimaginable that professional development would be one of the first items cut in a budget without considering the impact of such a decision on the quality of professional work, school goals, and student outcomes. Valuing learning also influences the recruitment and hiring of new teachers and administrators. As employers, school boards and administrators, guided by deeply held beliefs about learning, would look for educators who are lifelong learners and who see the link between their own learning and the learning of others. Finally, when professional learning is deeply valued, organizational change processes and the introduction of various innovations into schools would consider the learning needs of personnel required for successful implementation.

Valuing learning also requires educators to be explicit about its importance to high-quality teaching and learning. In professional learning communities, teachers and principals are lifelong learners who value their own learning and the learning of others. In contrast to more traditional work settings where professional improvement is individual and oftentimes completely unconnected to the learning and work of others, in professional learning cultures educators share knowledge through dialogue, consultation, reflective processes, and joint work. These processes help to reinforce explicit values around learning, strengthen individual and collective understanding of practice, and contribute to organizational improvement. One example of explicit valuing of learning can be found in descriptions of professional interactions at the Eagle Rock School in Estes Park, Colorado.[4] Here teachers use a tuner protocol process to share professional knowledge and foster dialogue through collaborative examination of student work.

Deep enough footings also require eight commitments. Anchored in values, these general commitments undergird professional learning communities in schools.

Professional Learning Communities

- Dedicate appropriate resources—time, money, materials, and personnel—for the enhancement of professional learning and practice.
- Integrate professional learning and work in ways that recognize the nature of professional work and its complexities.
- Foster individual autonomy and responsibility for professional growth and its connections to school priorities and student learning.
- Remove inhibitors and disincentives to learning and school improvement—including inflexible schedules, inappropriate reward structures, and cumbersome decision-making processes.
- Help teachers and principals deal effectively with contradictions, tensions and trade-offs that surround their own learning needs and their work with students.
- Provide assurance and security for learners as they take risks and cope with the uncertainties and stresses of changes in familiar routines in professional practice.
- Model and celebrate individual and collective learning.
- Remain steadfast in their commitments to schools as learning communities.

Figure 2.1, Site Survey: Commitment to Professional Learning, is an assessment tool for examining levels of individual and organizational commitment to professional learning. The eight items ask you to rate the professional learning environment in your school, district, or organization. The sum of the ratings for each item provides a level of commitment score. These scores describe perceptions of the depth of commitment to professional learning. These assessment data can be used to initiate dialogues about how to maintain or change those levels of commitment.

Deep enough footings are also grounded in moral purpose. Professional development for teachers and administrators is more than

Figure 2.1 Site Survey: Commitment to Professional Learning

Directions: For each indicator below, circle the number that best describes commitment to professional learning in your school. The following scale is used: 1 = not true; 2 = somewhat true; 3 = mostly true; 4 = very true.

Indicator of commitment	Not true	Somewhat true	Mostly true	Very true
1. There are adequate resources (time, money, materials, and personnel to support professional learning).	1	2	3	4
2. Professional learning is integrated into daily work.	1	2	3	4
3. Teachers and principals have autonomy in selecting professional development that connects with school goals and student learning.	1	2	3	4
4. Most disincentives and obstacles to professional learning have been eliminated or at least minimized.	1	2	3	4
5. People have the capacity to deal with contradictions in professional work and learning.	1	2	3	4
6. People know there is support when they try new things and take risks.	1	2	3	4
7. We are all learners and model learning for one another.	1	2	3	4
8. There is continuous support for professional learning and growth.	1	2	3	4

Give a concrete example to illustrate your rating: If commitment is rated high, indicate ways to maintain this level of commitment in your school. If commitment is rated low, indicate ways to improve the level of commitment in your school.

just the accumulation of new technical professional knowledge and skills to raise student test scores. The resources we dedicate to the ongoing learning of teachers and principals is an investment in their primary work—the care and development of children. Further, student learning and development are fundamental to our beliefs about the purposes of public education in a democratic society. Neil Postman describes this moral purpose:

> Schools contribute toward strengthening the spiritual basis of the American Creed. That is how Jefferson understood it, how Horace Mann understood it, and how John Dewey understood it. And, in fact, there is no other way to understand it. The question is not, Does or doesn't public schooling create a public? The question is, what kind of public does it create? A conglomerate of self-indulgent consumers? Angry, soulless, directionless masses? Indifferent, confused citizens? Or a public imbued with confidence, a sense of purpose, a respect for learning, and tolerance.[5]

Wide Enough

In building construction, footings are needed to distribute and support the weight of the building; to provide support and stability, footings need to be wide enough to help distribute the overall weight of the structure. Without wide enough footings, the building may sink, become unstable, or simply collapse. New designs for professional development in schools require footings that are wide enough to provide support and to give learning structures and processes stability. What makes footings wide enough in professional development? To begin, footings that are wide enough have distributive qualities that strengthen the entire foundation. Wide foundations are attentive to the diversity of learner needs in schools. There is recognition of important differences that affect professional learning. These include differences in individual capacity, learning styles, learning readiness, and career stages. The foundation for professional development needs to be wide enough to deal with multiple dimensions of educators' work—intellectual, interpersonal, organizational, and occupational. Wide footings also support professional development by recognizing the intersection of professional learning and work. There are, of course, practical constraints within teachers' and administrators' work days that limit opportunities for job-embedded learning. Nonetheless, the distribution of learning opportunities across various dimensions of professional work mitigates forces that often relegate learning to the margins of professional work and practice. Sustained professional development in content and pedagogy has been shown to have a significant impact on professional practices that influence student learning outcomes.[6] Finally, professional development that is wide enough attends to the totality of educators' learning needs, their hearts, minds, and souls, not just their technical expertise. Put another way, professional learning requires a foundation that includes the "what," "how," and "why" of professional knowledge and practice.

Durable Enough

To provide support over time, the footings must be made of durable materials. Stone, steel, and concrete are the materials used for buildings. In the context of professional development, it is important to point out that *durability* does not mean *rigidity*. It means strength over time. What are the materials that make the foundations for professional development durable over time? Adequate resources, especially time and money, are essential components of a new architecture for professional learning in schools. The investments in professional learning for school personnel are as vital to schools as research and development are to industry. Corporations rarely cut research and development in response to budget constraints. If they do, they know they are limiting their future. Similarly, the capricious cutting of professional development resources is short-sighted; professional development is essential to organizational quality. Any builder who cuts costs in a building project by purchasing and using cheaper materials knows from experience that the final structure is neither of high quality nor very durable.

Footings need to be able to withstand various stresses and forces in the environment. Depending on local conditions, frost heaving the ground, slippage, termites, rot, and decay are threats to the stability of any structure. Similarly, things that eat away at the core supports for high-quality professional learning in schools threaten the stability of professional development structures. For example, school districts often hijack time, space, and personnel commandeering them for organizational maintenance and information showers, not professional development and enhancement of practice. Legislative bodies, for example, frequently mandate requirements with little or no money to support their implementation including the training of personnel to deal with these changes. Shifting political climates that bring new goals and priorities create more change than improvement. Still another threat is public opinion about professional development activities in schools. It is not uncommon to hear people in the community refer to staff development as "another day off for teachers." In part, such reactions are not all that surprising given the disruptions in child care for children and their parents. Regardless of any inconveniences to parents, professional development is work. The collective knowledge and professional expertise of schools are also greatly affected by staffing changes through retirements and staff mobility. Last, organizational "termites," those cynics, resisters, saboteurs, and negaholics

Figure 2.2 Laying the Foundation: Four Levels of Action

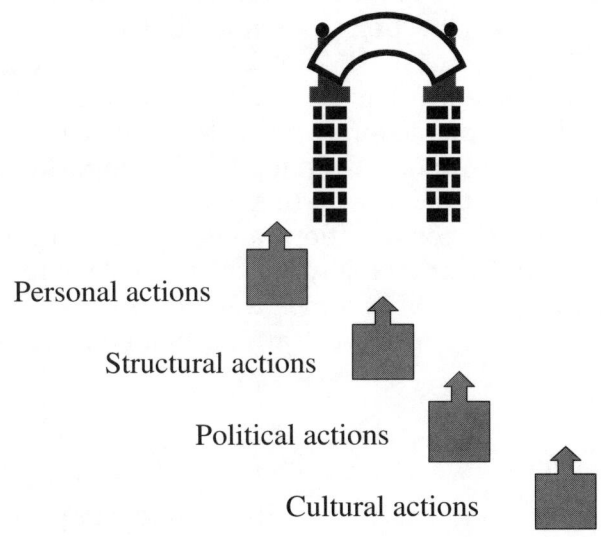

Personal actions

Structural actions

Political actions

Cultural actions

threaten the foundations of professional learning and community. Thus, the footings need to be made of materials generally resistant to their negative effects.

LAYING FOOTINGS IN PROFESSIONAL DEVELOPMENT THAT ARE DEEP, WIDE, AND DURABLE

It is one thing to know what to do in the area of professional development; it is quite another to know how to go about achieving desired outcomes. How does the idea of laying footings that are deep enough, wide enough, and durable enough apply to designs for professional learning? Figure 2.2 indicates four levels of action—personal, structural, political, and cultural—where teachers and administrators can apply their knowledge of solid foundations for professional learning in schools. Let's examine the practical implications of each for laying the foundations for a new architecture for professional development.

Personal Actions

We know from leadership and cultural studies that leaders communicate important organizational messages through their actions. How people behave, and what they spend their time doing, are much more powerful than what they say.[7] If you want to know what is important in terms of learning in schools, watch what teachers and administrators do, what they pay attention to, and what actions they reward. Now how does this play out in schools on a daily basis? If learning is truly valued, teachers and administrators are active learners themselves, and they make it a priority in their daily work and interactions in schools. They do not separate teaching and learning. As learners, they model the importance of learning for students and colleagues in "who they are" and "what they do." They engage others in explicit conversations about ideas and possibilities that animate their lives and work. Finally, professionals take responsibility for their own learning. Part of what it means to be a professional is to recognize one's obligation to continuous learning that enhances expertise and practice.

Creating Structures

Creating an environment that nurtures and supports professional learning requires careful attention to structural features both in and beyond schools. We know, for example, that many school environments optimize opportunities for learning by providing physical, psychological, and professional space for all staff. Because professional work experience is such a powerful component of professional learning, creating opportunities for teachers and administrators to learn while on the job is critical. Thus, restructuring time within busy school days is vitally important to professional growth. Teachers and principals need time to meet, talk, and reflect on their practice and its impact on student learning. In terms of physical space and materials, this includes such obvious things as personal space (desks and offices), available computers and other tools for communication, and physical space (work rooms, conference/meeting rooms, and labs) where professionals can interact on a daily basis. These are minimal work conditions for professionals in business and other fields. Unfortunately, far too many educators work in impoverished professional work settings. For instance, it is not uncommon in schools to find teachers and principals sitting at tables meant for children, meeting in hallways, being relegated to lounges when their classrooms are being used, and organizing opportunities outside of school to find time to work together.[8] These are hardly optimal conditions for professional work, let alone continuous learning.

If professional development is an essential part of professional work, then such supports as time (during the work day, week, and year), appropriate materials, personnel, and financial resources also need to be in place. However, even when there are adequate financial resources to support comprehensive staff development programs in school, finding time continues to be a major challenge. A number of school districts around the country have found creative ways to carve out time to support professional learning.[9] Scheduling common planning time, hiring substitutes to free teachers for collaborative work, adding contract days in the summer, and restructuring the starting and ending times of the school days are frequently used to create time for professional learning.

Providing incentives, removing barriers to professional growth, and implementing an assessment system are structural features that support professional learning in schools. Schools and communities need to create an incentive system that encourages and supports professional growth and development. Incentives include increased pay and benefits, career advancement, recognition and awards, study leaves, and job enrichment, to name a few. What is important is that the incentive system aligns individual and collective professional learning, school/district goals and priorities, student and community needs, and various extrinsic and intrinsic rewards. Experiments in school districts around the nation are illustrative of the ways school districts are attempting to link system incentives and to professional learning.[10] Removing inhibitors and disincentives to learning is another structural action that supports the development of professional learning environments. Builders remove debris or other obstacles before laying the footing. In schools, "cleaning the site" may include such actions as dropping daily schedules that impede professional learning, changing union contract language to permit opportunities for feedback through formative evaluation through peer coaching and mentoring of novice teachers, and changing the decision processes and structures for the allocation of resources to support professional development. Designers of staff development also need to consider removing any obstacles to laying the foundations for professional learning in schools. Finally, the implementation of an assessment system that provides continuous feedback on learning processes and outcomes is critical.

Creating a Learning Culture

In her research on successful schools, Rosenholtz described two types of schools—struck schools and thriving schools.[11] This dichotomy describes a range of cultural dimensions that support or undermine a healthy and positive learning environment in a school. Culture, often defined as the way things are done within an organization, includes values, norms, and practices that characterize the essence of an organization.[12] Thriving professional learning communities are cultures in which learning is the driving force of the organization. The use of symbols, ceremonies, rituals, and traditions are among the ways learning communities express their values around professional learning and practice. For example, in learning communities, both learners and learning outcomes are *celebrated* in award ceremonies, displays, and special events at public meetings. They also *recognize* and honor learners and learner outcomes, *showcase* learning activities (action research conferences, networks, and poster sessions), *develop norms* for sharing professional knowledge, *support* collaborative inquiry and learning experiences, and *deprivatize* practice.[13]

Norms of professionalism permeate the professional learning community. Knowledge and expertise are part of collective professional capacity, not individual status. Teachers, principals, and other staff deprivatize their practice through collaborative inquiry and learning, joint work, engaging in reflective dialogues, peer support, and mentoring. Each of these provide professional, psychological, and personal support for teachers and administrators experiencing the risks and rewards of professional learning and changes in professional routines and practice.

Developing Political Support

Developing political support for new designs for professional development requires political awareness and skill. New designs for professional learning break the mold and often require significant changes in structures and routines. Thus, garnering political support calls for school leaders who understand professional learning and can explain its importance to others—school board members, community leaders, parents, and other stakeholders who may have questions or concerns. The politics of professional development also involves competition for scarce resources in schools, districts, and beyond. Clarity of purpose, networking with key decision makers, and persistence create and sustain a broad base of support for the professional learning community. The political environment of schools includes unions and negotiated contracts. Schools boards and teacher unions have negotiated contracts for salary and benefits. More recently, various school reform and improvement initiatives have forced these parties to reexamine their agreements with special attention to hours and conditions of employment. Though localized and generally limited, the use of joint committees, trust agreements, and contract waivers is emerging as new mechanisms for teachers' unions and school districts to seek common ground to deal with mutual interest and benefit, professional development included.[14]

Table 2.1, Assessing Levels of Action, is a site survey for examining levels and types of actions that lay the foundation for professional development in your school. Specifically, the survey poses questions in each of the four critical levels of actions needed to lay deep, wide, and durable foundations for professional development.

DEFINING PROFESSIONAL DEVELOPMENT

Like many of you, I have had difficulty at times understanding the differences among such terms as *professional development, continuing professional education, staff development, inservice, human resource development,* and *training.* I believe part of the confusion may be the result of these terms being used interchangeably, with little regard for conceptual or practical

Table 2.1 Site Survey: Assessing Levels of Action

The following questions ask you to reflect on levels of action that lay the foundation for professional development in your school.

Personal Actions
- In what way(s) do I demonstrate that I value professional learning in my work?
- Do I model learning for my students? For my colleagues?
- How frequently do I discuss new ideas and things I've learned with my colleagues?
- Do I take responsibility for my own professional learning?

Creating Structures
- In what way(s) have we worked to make professional learning an important aspect of professional work?
- Do we create adequate time for teachers and staff to meet, talk, and reflect on their learning?
- How does the physical environment in our school affect teachers' and administrators' professional learning?
- What are the most powerful incentives that support professional learning?
- What barriers, if any, are there to professional learning? How do we deal with them?

Creating a Learning Culture
- How would a visitor to our school know that professional learning is a valued part of our professional culture?
- What symbols, ceremonies, and traditions celebrate professional learning?
- How is professional knowledge shared?
- What practices in our school support and/or enhance professional learning?
- Are there any negative aspects of culture that limit professional learning?

Political Actions
- In what way(s) do leaders in our school generate public support for professional development?
- What mechanisms are used to keep the community informed about professional development issues?
- What opportunities are there for teachers and administrators to tell others about professional development?
- What role does the local teachers' association play in the design, delivery, and evaluation of professional development?
- What partnerships between school professionals and community leaders exist for ongoing professional development opportunities?

Figure 2.3   Defining Professional Development

Learning opportunities

Professional
Development

Improved practice

Creative/reflective
engagement

differences. On a practical level, it is difficult, for example, to determine whether an after-school session for teachers is training, inservice, staff development, or organizational maintenance. And, does it make any difference what an activity is called? Is it possible that reading a book, listening to a lecture, observing a colleague teach, conducting an action research project, and keeping a reflective journal might all be professional development activities?

To bring greater clarity to what I mean by the term professional development used in this book, I developed a definition grounded in research, personal experience, and current literature:

> Professional development refers to learning opportunities
> that engage educators' creative and reflective capacities
> in ways that strengthen their practice.

There are three important concepts embedded in this definition—*learning opportunities, engagement of creative and reflective capacities,* and *improved practice* (see Figure 2.3). Next I describe in greater detail how each of these concepts contributes to the definition of professional development.

Learning Opportunities

A primary criterion for determining whether or not an activity qualifies as professional development is that it involves learning opportunities. As obvious as this may seem, staff developers, administrators, teachers, and a virtual cottage industry of educational consultants ignore this principle every day. Test this assertion against your experiences in schools. Have you ever been involved in a staff development planning meeting where one or more of the following things occurred?

- A faculty member returns from a professional conference where she heard an inspiring speaker and suggests getting him for the next scheduled inservice day in the spring.
- The principal, who has been taking a course at the university, decides to buy everyone on the staff a copy of a book that stimulated great discussions during class.
- A corporate management team offers, at no cost to the school, a series of leadership training seminars over the following year for all administrators and teacher leaders.
- A group of teachers participated in a "ropes" training course and they recommend scheduling a one-day course for the faculty to begin the following school year.
- The school board mandates training all staff on procedures for dealing with hostage and gun violence in the schools.

Each of these has the potential to be an important learning opportunity for teachers and principals in a school. Many times, however, professional development planners weigh more heavily the convenience and opportunity dimensions of various activities than explicit learning outcomes aligned with staff, school, and community needs and priorities. What we know about learning is not always applied to professional development. "Much of what constitutes the typical approach to formal teacher professional development is antithetical to what promotes teacher learning."[15] The key dimension, often assumed but not explicitly stated, is that learning, not the activity, is the focus of professional development experiences. Thus, learning opportunities are more than interesting activities, special events, or scheduled inservice days on the school calendar. New designs for professional learning must be grounded in what we know about how people learn, especially how teachers and principals learn. The current body of research on learning suggests that the design of learning environments affects professional learning processes, the transfer of knowledge, and application of that knowledge into practice.

Engagement

Professional learning opportunities that engage teachers' and principals' creative and reflective capacities have the greatest potential to influence their practice. The professional knowledge base of educators is fundamentally conditional. That is, an educator's expert knowledge cannot be reduced to a set of isolated skills and bits of technical knowledge. Instead, professional expertise is determined by how knowledge and skills are applied in situations of practice. As any teacher will tell you, a math lesson that worked well with one group of students may not be successful with another group. It is not because the teacher's knowledge and skills have suddenly diminished; a new mix of students and setting requires the teacher to use his knowledge and skills in ways that meet the demands of the new situation, not in simple replication of previous practice.

Thus, in any learning situation, teachers and principals are intent on learning the content or the skills presented but always with an eye toward how they might be used in practice. Learning opportunities should be designed in ways that tap into educators' natural inclination to reflect on, personalize, and transform new knowledge and skills to fit their personal style and demands of daily practice. Despite efforts by policy makers and educational reformers to make teaching and school leadership more scientific, the work of teachers and principals is more like art than science. As practitioners, they "struggle to adjust and readjust, to develop routines, and to establish patterns, only to recast what has been done in a new form to meet a new need or a new vision." Like the craftsman, their work is "messy and a highly personalized enterprise, for it concerns itself with the making and remaking of an object until it satisfies the standards of its creator."[16]

Improved Practice

The primary purpose of professional development for teachers and principals is to improve their practice. Though seemingly obvious, I believe it is important to emphasize this point. Schlecty and Whitford provide a general framework for examining professional development activities.[17] They describe three general functions that can be served by a professional development activity. The first function is an *establishment function*—promoting organizational change through the implementation of new programs, technologies, or systems in schools. A second function is *organizational maintenance*—emphasizing compliance with mandates and focusing primarily on administrative and organizational goals. Finally, there is the *enhancement function*, that is, improved professional practice.

While the establishment and maintenance functions are important in schools, it is the enhancement function—improved professional practice—that I focus on in this book. I do so for several reasons. First, there is substantial evidence that the quality of teachers' and principals' professional practice greatly affects student learning. Each year we invest billions of dollars on professional development to update educators' knowledge and skills. This investment is made primarily because we believe that the best way to improve the educational outcomes of all children is to provide knowledgeable and skilled educational professionals to work with them. Second, I believe much of the negative reaction to traditional inservice meetings and workshops, expressed as resistance, boredom, or general cynicism, comes from feelings of being powerless and used. Participants in traditional staff development have felt powerless because others have made decisions about the content and delivery of the professional development activities. Participants feel used because resources spent on activities focused on organizational maintenance or compliance functions are robbing them of the time and money to needed to support their professional needs.

It is disingenuous to call a session on compliance with administrative rules professional development. It hides the real purpose of the session by cloaking it in the legitimacy of professional development clothes.

Let us go back to a question I posed earlier. Is it possible that reading a book, listening to a lecture, observing a colleague teach, conducting an action research project, and reflective journaling are all professional development activities? If the activity presents a learning opportunity that engages educators' creative and reflective capacities in ways that strengthen their professional practice, the answer is an unequivocal, Yes! If these criteria are not met, I do not deny the legitimacy of the activity per se. I simply would not refer to it as professional development.

CONCLUSION

The integrity of new designs for professional learning rests on foundations that provide support and stability over time. Like their counterparts in physical architecture, new designs for professional development are supported by *deep*, core values and commitment to learning, by *wide* support at the intersection of educators' work and professional growth (intellectual, interpersonal, organizational, and occupational), and by *durable* attributes expressed in four levels of action—personal actions, creating structures, creating learning cultures, and developing political support. These elements are the foundation for professional development—*learning opportunities that engage educators' creative and reflective capacities in ways that strengthen their practice.*

SITE VISITS

www.ed.gov/inits/teachers/eisenhower/
Online version of Designing effective professional development: Lessons from the Eisenhower Program (1999).
www.nsdc.org
National Staff Development Council Standards for Staff Development homepage.
www.ncrel.org/pd/
Among the many resources available at this site is Professional development: Learning from the best: A toolkit for schools and districts based on the National Awards Program for Model Professional Development.

SUPPLEMENTARY READING

Hassel, E. (1999). *Professional development: Learning from the best.* Oak Brook, IL: North Central Regional Educational Laboratory.
Lieberman, A., & Miller, L. (1990). Revisiting the social realities of teaching. In A. Lieberman & L. Miller (Eds.), *Staff development for education in the 90s.* New York: Teachers College Press.

National Education Association. *Time strategies*. (1994). Washington, DC: Author.
Rosenholtz, S. (1989). *Teachers' workplace: The social organization of schools*. White
Plains, NY: Longman.

NOTES

1. Thoreau, D. (1906). *The writing of Henry David Thoreau* (Vol. 2). Boston: Houghton Mifflin, 356.

2. See Professional development: Learning from the best. Retrieved July 1, 2002, from www.ncrel.org

3. See Designing effective professional development: Lessons from the Eisenhower Program (1999). Retrieved July 1, 2002, from www.ed.gov/inits/teachers/eisenhower/; National Staff Development Council Standards for Staff Development, retrieved July 1, 2002 from www.nsdc.org; Hawley, W.D., & Valli, L. (1999). The essentials of effective professional development: A new consensus. In L. Darling-Hammond & G. Sykes (Eds.), *Teaching as the learning profession: Handbook of policy and practice*. San Francisco: Jossey-Bass.

4. Easton, L. B. (2002). How the tuning protocol works. *Educational Leadership*. *59*(6), 28–30.

5. Postman, N. (1995). *The end of education: Redefining the value of school*. New York: Knopf, 18.

6. See Designing effective professional development: Lessons from the Eisenhower Program (1999). Retrieved July 1, 2002, from www.ed.gov/inits/teachers/eisenhower/

7. Schein, E. H. (1985). *Organizational culture and leadership*. San Francisco: Jossey-Bass.

8. Bredeson, P. V., & Scribner, J. P. (2000). *A state-wide professional development conference: Useful strategy for learning or inefficient use of resources?* Retrieved July 1, 2002, from http://epaa.asu.edu/epaa/v8n13html

9. National Education Association. (1994). *Time strategies*. Washington, DC: Author.

10. Odden, A., & Kelley, C. (2001). *Paying teachers for what they know and do: New and smarter compensation strategies to improve schools* (2nd ed.). Thousand Oaks, CA: Corwin Press.

11. Rosenholtz, S. J. (1989). *Teachers' workplace: The social organization of schools*. White Plains, NY: Longman.

12. Deal, T., & Peterson, K. D. (1999). *Shaping school culture: The heart of leadership*. San Francisco: Jossey-Bass.

13. Hassel, E. (1999). *Professional development: Learning from the best*. Oak Brook, IL: North Central Regional Educational Laboratory.

14. Bredeson, P. V. (2001). Negotiated learning: Union contracts and teacher professional development. Retrieved July 1, 2002, from http://epaa.asu.edu/epaa/v9n26.html

15. Bransford, J. D., Brown, A. L., & Cocking, R. C. (Eds.). (1999). *How people learn: Brain, mind, experience and school*. Washington, DC: National Academy Press.

16. Lieberman, A., & Miller, L. (1990). Revisiting the social realities of teaching. In A. Lieberman & L. Miller (Eds.), *Staff development for education in the '90s*. New York: Teachers College Press, 95.

17. Schlecty, P. C., & Whitford, B. L. (1983). The organizational context of school systems and the functions of staff development. In G. A. Griffin (Ed.), *Staff development: 82nd yearbook of the NSSE* (pp. 62–91). Chicago: University of Chicago Press.

3

Creating a Professional Learning Community

A true community is only able to grow and strengthen itself by including all of its members and finding room for them to develop their capacities within its own pattern of growth.[1]

INTRODUCTION

Eric Hoffer, the American longshoreman philosopher, captured the essence of a professional learning community. "In a time of drastic change it is the learners who inherit the earth. The learned usually find themselves equipped to deal with a world that no longer exists."[2] In this chapter, we examine the importance of learning in schools. Obvious as this may seem to most educators, our experiences suggest that schools at times can be more about teaching than learning, more about discipline than development, more about competition than community, and more about programs than professional development. In particular we turn our attention to an examination of practices and conditions that support effective learning for everyone in the schools—students and staff. The new architecture for professional development is about creating learning spaces for educators. These spaces, however, are not isolated, self-contained spaces; they are ones that support individual growth, foster collaborative learning, and build collective capacity. I begin the chapter with a review of literature describing the term, professional learning community, highlighting its three interdependent dimensions. Next, using two major strands of scholarly work—learning communities and organizational learning—I identify common characteristics across these works and describe tools for creating professional learning communities in schools. The chapter concludes with a discussion of the "unlearning organization." Though I believe the reader will think this is a contradiction to the first two sections, I make the case that the process of unlearning (organized abandonment) is critical to the creation of professional learning communities.

PROFESSIONAL LEARNING COMMUNITY: WHAT IS IT?

The concept of a professional learning community in schools has swept across the field of education like a prairie fire fanned by the winds of educational reform and school improvement. Dozens of scholars and practitioners have used the metaphor of community to describe the link between professional learning, student achievement, and school improvement. There is no shortage of interpretations, descriptions, and definitions of the concept of professional learning community in the literature. Here's a sample from leading scholars:

- Coral Mitchell and Larry Sackney—"A learning community consists of a group of people who take an active, reflective, collaborative, learning-oriented, and growth-promoting approach toward both the mysteries and the problems of teaching and learning."[3]

- Roland Barth—"All teachers and administrators can learn. I believe these words will become a reality when we transform the schoolhouse into a community of learners, a culture of adaptability, continuous experimentation, and invention."[4]

- Michelle Collay, Diane Dunlap, Walter Enloe, and George W. Gagnon Jr.—"Learning circles are small communities of learners among teachers and others who come together intentionally for the purpose of supporting each other in the process of learning."[5]

- Thomas J. Sergiovanni—"A covenantal community is a group of people who share certain purposes, values, and beliefs, who a feel a strong sense of place, and who think of the welfare of the group as being more important than that of the individual."[6]

- Ernest Boyer—"The school becomes a *community for learning* when it is a purposeful place; a communicative place, a just place, a disciplined place, a caring place, and a celebrative place."[7]

- Peter Senge—"A professional learning community is one that continually expands its capacities to adjust to new realities, create new structures and processes that move people and the organization to higher levels of performance."[8]

What is apparent from this small sample from the literature is that each author defines the concept of professional learning community somewhat differently. Whether the perspective highlights aspects of values and culture, relationships, actions, purpose, or organizational structures and processes, each contributes important dimensions to our collective understanding of the professional learning community. For instance, Mitchell and Sackney anchor their definition in the context of teaching and learning, describing how practitioners collaboratively and reflexively confront the challenges and contradictions in their daily work. Barth highlights the cultural dimensions of learning communities guided by powerful norms of creativity, continuous experimentation, and adaptability. Collay, Dunlap, Enloe, and Gagnon view learning communities as nested learning circles created by small groups of individuals in schools and other organizations to support individual and collective learning. Sergiovanni invokes the idea that communities are sacred enterprises among individuals who in their interactions create a shared sense of purpose and professional meaning. Boyer uses the concept of place—physical, emotional, and psychological—to describe the concept of the professional learning community, a place with a shared sense of mission, purpose, history, and collaborative practice. Senge emphasizes the importance of continually expanding individual, collective, and school capacities—knowledge, skills, and performance competence. This expansion of professional and school capacities is critical to teachers and administrators as they make various adjustments by creating new structures and processes to support changes in their practice that enhance learning and work in the school.

To some readers, the richness and diversity of perspectives noted earlier may suggest a lack of consensus around the concept of "professional learning community." I believe these differences enrich the concept and help us understand more clearly what we mean when we use the words *professional*, *learning*, and *community*. Drawing on the literature, let's examine the meaning of each dimension separately. Figure 3.1 represents the three interdependent dimensions that are particularly important to new designs for professional learning in schools.

Professional: More Than a License

When we use the term *professional* to describe an educator, we are essentially describing a set of unique characteristics based on training, knowledge, and skills a person possesses. Based on a unique set of competencies anchored in expert knowledge and skills, states issue professional licenses

Figure 3.1 Professional Learning Community

Professional

Learning

Community

to educators to practice thereby according them particular privileges and responsibilities. The state has an interest in high-quality service to children and adults. A professional license is a mechanism for ensuring quality and for protecting clients from harmful or fraudulent practices.

What exactly does the title of professional certify? In general, this means the educator—teacher, counselor, or administrator—has participated in an extended period of training and preparation in which he/she has demonstrated, through a variety of measures, advanced knowledge, skills, and performance competencies. This includes such areas as the psychology of learning, teaching methodologies, understanding of human growth and development, and specialized content knowledge. Professional educators are also guided by a code of ethics centered in the care and nurture of students. Their choices and daily practice focus on meeting the cognitive, social, emotional, and developmental needs of their students. The code of ethics also commits educators to high standards of practice, respect for the privacy and confidentiality of child and family information, social justice, and equity. As licensed professionals, educators have an obligation to review and self-monitor their professional practice periodically. Professional self-assessment also includes a felt obligation to reflect on experience, expand one's repertoire of practice, and develop greater professional expertise. Beyond personal development, professionals also have an obligation to contribute to organizational quality and improvement.

Another dimension of professionalism is autonomy, that is, relative freedom from interference with daily practice and professional judgments. However, there are a number of constraints, which I describe briefly below, that attenuate educators' professional autonomy. Within legal, ethical, and standards of practice boundaries, professional educators have relative autonomy to make choices that best serve their students and govern their work. Commitment to high standards of practice also requires a professional to be open to learning and improvement. Thus, ongoing reflection on one's practice and its outcomes is a hallmark of being a professional.

Constraints on Professionalism

When compared to the work of other professionals—for example, physicians, accountants, and dentists—educators' professional work is constrained in a number of unique ways. To begin, state governments have historically exercised considerable political and administrative control over teachers, administrators, and schools. The sheer numbers required to operate a public system of education in a nation with 285 million people are daunting to any professional group. In 1998–1999 there were 16,542 public school districts, operating more than 92,000 schools, with 2.9 million teachers serving 47.4 million students.[9] Thus, the profession's ability to control standards for the recruitment, training, entry, and ongoing professional education of practitioners is severely limited. Finally, the complexity of teaching and learning has also presented educators with challenges in articulating a distinctive and generally agreed-upon knowledge base that guides professional practice. There is a significant body of research that supports successful practice. However, the dissemination of this research and successful implementation of practices that reflect this knowledge base have proven difficult. The idea of taking new knowledge and professional practices to scale continues to frustrate researchers and policy makers.

Learning

The organizations that will truly excel in the future will be the organizations that discover how to tap people's commitment and capacity to learn at *all* levels in an organization.[10]

It is ironic that much of what we know from research about the factors and conditions that promote effective student learning is often ignored when it comes to the adults who work in schools. Though there are important distinctions between the learning of children and professionals in schools, the general principles of human cognition apply to all learners. So what are some of things we know about learning? To what degree are principles of human cognition evident in the design, delivery, content, and assessment of professional learning in schools?

There is a substantial body of research that describes how people learn, what conditions best support their learning, and how current knowledge contributes to knowledge transfer and future learning.[11] I have selected a small sample of findings on cognition and learning cited in current reviews of research. As you read each one, ask yourself the following

Principles of Cognition

- Different kinds of learning goals require different approaches to instruction.
- Effective instruction begins with understanding what learners bring to the learning opportunity—prior knowledge, beliefs, experiences, and culture.
- Learners are most successful if they understand how they learn and think.
- All new learning involves transfer. Prior knowledge can help or hinder the understanding of new information.
- All learning takes place in settings that have particular sets of cultural and social norms and expectations that influence learning and transfer.
- Learners are motivated to spend the time needed to learn complex subjects and to solve problems that they find interesting.

Table 3.1   Learning Principles: Implications for Professional Development in Practice

Learning Principle	Implication for Professional Development
Different learning goals require different instructional strategies	Learning outcomes identified before content, delivery, assessments designed
Understanding learner's prior knowledge, beliefs, experiences, and culture	Ongoing assessment of learner needs and knowledge
Successful learners understand how they learn	Critical reflection and meta-cognition built in to learning activities
Learning involves transfer	Time, resources, and personnel provided for learner to move ideas into practice
Learning environments influence learning outcomes and transfer	Professional learning is on-site and job-embedded
Motivated learners spend required time to learn task or solve problem	Professional development practices are anchored in learner's interest and practice

questions. How do professional development opportunities in my school reflect principles of effective learning? What would an architecture of professional development reflecting these principles look like in practice?

Table 3.1 illustrates how each of these principles guides the new architecture for professional development in practice.

Of course, we know a great deal more about cognition than what is in these six bulleted statements. These findings and others guide educators' professional practice in the design of optimal learning environments that promote student learning and success. It is reasonable to think these fundamental understandings of human cognition would undergird designs for professional learning in schools.

Community

Recently there has been renewed interest in the concept of community. Robert Putnam, in his article, "Bowling Alone: America's Declining Social Capital," described macro-shifts in the United States that have eroded the sense of community and thus endanger our democratic society historically rooted in its collective capacity to form associations.[12] He argues that America is witnessing a decline in social activism and civic participation. He cites precipitous drops in memberships in such traditional social, civic, and fraternal organizations as the PTA, the League of Women voters, service clubs, and churches. Other scholars disagree with Putnam's assessment of social capital in the United States. They argue that civic participation is not declining; it is simply changing into more diverse and loosely structured associations that reflect the realities of contemporary society. Regardless of the interpretation of these shifts in civic participation, both sides agree that the development and spirit of community are essential to the health and long-term success of any organization or society.

Concepts of Community

The term community refers to a number of different types of social connections. There are communities based on the relationships among people, such as families and fraternal organizations. There are communities of place—neighborhoods and villages—where individuals share a common locale and develop a sense of identity. The sense of community can also be the product of shared ideas, values, and goals as exemplified in the drive that energizes volunteer workers who renovate housing in blighted, impoverished areas. Etienne Wenger offers another view of community. He argues that "engagement in social practice is the fundamental process by which we learn and become who we are."[13] As people negotiate and create meaning through formal and informal channels of interaction over time, they form various communities as well as their identities in them.

Schools as Communities

In many ways, each of these types of communities can be reflected in schools. However, professional learning communities do not emerge automatically just because students, teachers, and administrators work side-by-side and share a common schedule. As noted earlier in the chapter,

Figure 3.2 Elements of Responsive Community

> Wholeness that welcomes diversity
>
> Strong core values
>
> Mutual trust and care
>
> Teamwork and participation
>
> Affirmation

Ernest Boyer reminds us what it takes to forge a real school community. "To become a true community the institution must be organized around people. . . . What we are really talking about is the culture of school, the vision that is shared, the way people relate to one another. . . . Simply stated, the school becomes a community for learning when it is a purposeful place; a communicative place, a just place, a discipline place, a caring, place, and a celebrative place."[14]

John Gardner's work describing the *responsive community* provides another framework for understanding schools as professional communities.[15] Figure 3.2 represents five elements of responsive communities.

A POWERFUL COMBINATION: PROFESSIONAL-LEARNING-COMMUNITY

What would it mean if norms of professionalism, principles of learning, and attributes of community were brought together? What would it mean for schools? What influence would it have on the architecture for professional development in those schools? Figure 3.3 represents two possibilities, among many, that might characterize schools as professional learning communities. The degree of overlap among the three dimensions visually

Vignette of a Responsive School Community

Let us imagine a responsive school community that authentically expresses these elements in its daily work. It would be a school where wholeness welcomes diversity by nurturing an open climate for dissent, respecting individual identity within the whole, and dealing with conflict effectively. In this school, organizational vision, purpose, and practice are anchored in strong core values. These values are routinely reassessed against vision, purpose, and outcomes of practice. In a responsive school community, there are powerful social norms of trust, care, teamwork, and commitment to children and their learning. The attribute of participation means everyone in the school feels a sense of belonging and believes that he/she makes important contributions to the school community's wholeness and success. The sense of belonging is reinforced through affirmation of shared commitment, moral purpose, and collective capacity.

This is not an imaginary school! There are hundreds of schools across the country where these elements are not theoretical possibilities; they are daily realities of their life in community.

describes the depth and pervasiveness of attributes of a professional learning community (PLC). The diagram on the left of the figure indicates that some elements of a professional learning community exist in the organization. Differences in the size of overlapping circles in the Venn diagram represent differences in the depth and intensity of attributes of a PLC. The small amount of overlap in the diagram on the left indicates that attributes of PLC remain at the margins of the organization's culture. In contrast, the diagram on the right illustrates both in the size of the circles and in the significant overlap among the three dimensions that attributes of professionalism, learning, and community are powerful dimensions that shape the culture of this organization. Bringing the three dimensions together is part of the work of professional development architect-practitioners. The good news is that there are wonderful examples of educational practitioners who are creating PLCs in their schools.

Strategies for Building a Professional Learning Community

Deborah Meier, former director of Central Park East Schools in New York, believes that a major role for school leaders is to create a climate in schools that fosters the development of mental and moral habits among students and staff to build and sustain a successful school community. These habits of mind and professional practice include the capacity to deal

Figure 3.3 Two Contrasting Images of Professional Learning Community

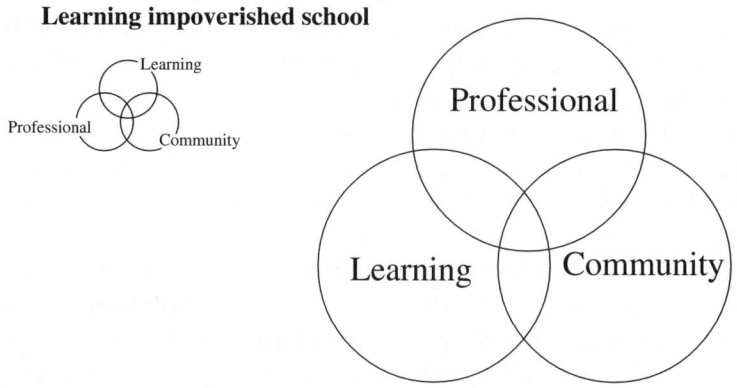

with the uncertainties and ambiguities in teaching and learning with the ability to act confidently on partial knowledge. As professionals, teachers and principals must also be open to new ideas, views, and possibilities for improvement in their practice, even when it requires substantial changes. Meier also believes strong professional community requires individuals to have a general inclination to step into the shoes of others.[16]

Researchers and organizational development specialists also suggest strategies for educators working to create PLC.[17] The hard work of designing and maintaining a professional learning community requires a clear and focused mission, one that gives meaning and identity to the passion, commitment, and energies for building and sustaining the community over time. PLCs must also have coherent instructional programs supported by professional development, a strong professional culture, and decision-making structures. With active and supportive parents, these learning communities have developed systems of accountability, primarily informal, that link together in meaningful ways performance standards, assessment strategies, and consequences based on performance. Finally, leadership is important to the development and success of a PLC. Highly effective leaders understand and creatively use the natural organizational tensions between the forces of centralization and decentralization. They are true entrepreneurs who work collaboratively to keep the focus on teaching and learning while consistently handling the nuts of bolts of management. This includes such enabling conditions as autonomy over their budgets, personnel decisions, school governance, and curriculum and links to and support from other networks and organizations.[18]

Two important lines of scholarly work also help us understand ways to build professional learning communities. The first is the body of works on *learning communities*. The second comes from Peter Senge's extensive work on *organizational learning*. Each suggests critical skills needed to create professional learning communities in schools.

Professional learning communities are dynamic creations of the people who work in them. "A learning community consists of a group of people who take an active, reflective, collaborative, learning-oriented, and growth-promoting approach toward both the mysteries and the problems of teaching and learning."[19] Mitchell and Sackney, for instance, describe three pivotal capacities (skills) that educators must develop if they want to create a true learning community in their school. First, educators must develop *personal capacity*. Personal capacity involves deep and critical deconstruction and reconstruction of individual professional knowledge and practice. Second, *interpersonal capacity* fosters collegial relations and collective practices whereby professional learning becomes a sacred norm for the group. Third, *organizational capacity* requires educators to develop and build structures and systems that support and value individual learning while facilitating collective learning. Individual, group, and organizational capacities build on each other and are mutually reinforcing. PLCs nurture and support all learners—staff and students. Barth describes the symbiotic relationship among all learners by comparing teachers and administrators to passengers on airplanes. As passengers, they routinely are informed that if oxygen masks should appear during the flight, they should put their own mask on first before trying to assist a child with them. The same is true for learning in schools. "Principals, preoccupied with expected outcomes, desperately want teachers to breathe in new ideas, yet are not themselves visible, voracious learners. Teachers badly want their students to learn, yet seldom reveal themselves as learners to children. All teachers and administrators can learn. I believe these words will become a reality when we transform the schoolhouse into a community of learners, a culture of adaptability, continuous experimentation, and invention. Only when the schoolhouse becomes a context for adult development will it become hospitable to student development."[20]

Senge's work on organizational learning provides another set of powerful tools for building professional learning communities. These tools are grounded in five disciplines, or bodies of theory and technique, that must be studied and mastered in order to be put into practice effectively. The five disciplines are *systems thinking*, *personal mastery*, *mental models*, *shared vision*, and *team learning*. At this point, I provide only abbreviated descriptions of each from Senge:

- *Systems thinking* refers to deep understanding of the underlying patterns and recurring themes that characterize the relationships among individual parts and the whole.
- *Personal mastery* is the discipline of continually clarifying and deepening our personal vision, of focusing our energies, of developing patience, and of seeing reality objectively.

- *Mental models* are deeply ingrained assumptions, generalizations, or even pictures or images that influence how we understand the world and how we take action.
- *Shared vision* involves the skills of revealing in multiple ways pictures of the future that foster genuine collective commitment and enrollment rather than compliance.
- *Team learning*, the fundamental learning unit in modern organizations, starts with dialogue, the capacity of members of a team to suspend assumptions and enter into a genuine thinking, knowing, and doing together.[21]

The five disciplines support active learning at all levels in schools—individual, group, and organizational. Learning how and when to use these tools affords educators the opportunity to build learning communities that reflect their purposes, core values, and unique characteristics.

ASSESSING ATTRIBUTES OF PROFESSIONAL LEARNING COMMUNITY

Given what we know about PLCs and the strategies educators are using to move their schools toward becoming more authentic learning communities, it is important to have tools for assessing the degree to which your school embodies the attributes of a professional learning community. Some of the most sustained and important work on measuring attributes of professional learning community has been done by Shirley Hord and colleagues at the Southwest Educational Development Laboratory.[22] The School Professional Staff Learning Community survey is a 17-item assessment that helps teachers and principals evaluate their schools against commonly identified attributes of successful professional learning communities. Using the survey provides valuable self-assessment data for planning organizational change focused on the development of a professional learning community. Using these data helps addresses the following questions. What are your school's strongest attributes as a professional learning community? Where is improvement needed? How would your assessment of attributes of PLC compare to the assessment of professional colleagues? If there are differences, what might account for them? How might you use this information to build a professional learning community? The assessment tool provides staff an opportunity to describe their sense of professional community in concrete ways that others can understand. When individual ratings and examples are aggregated and used as the basis for collaborative discussions, they offer individual, group, and organizational snapshots of a professional learning community. Information generated in this assessment also provides a guide to school improvement and planning processes.

The Unlearning School Community

There is an intriguing paradox that accompanies the creation of a learning community. In the process of becoming a true learning community, people need to develop the capacity at all levels to systematically unlearn (abandon) unproductive or outmoded structures, processes, routines, practices, and ways of thinking. The most successful educators in the 21st century will be those who help their organizations develop skills and capacities for "unlearning" and strategic abandonment. Though it seems contradictory to discuss the importance of organizational unlearning in the same chapter as creating a professional learning community, let us examine briefly the notion of organizational unlearning.

Gardeners and horticulturists have long known that healthy growth and productivity from plants often require judicious and thoughtful pruning. Like grapevines and raspberry bushes, schools as learning organizations require careful attention to branches and stocks that no longer contribute to their productivity. This principle seems obvious, yet pruning and unlearning in schools are generally more complex and difficult than tasks carried out in gardens. We return to the metaphor of architecture; the processes of unlearning are comparable to clearing debris from the building site.

So what happens if educators do not learn to use systematically the principles of unlearning? The cost can be very high personally and professionally. For instance, teachers and administrators will likely waste energy and time, fail to reach goals, work more for less, and ultimately be unprepared for new realities and challenges confronting them. Ask yourself, what have I stopped doing within the last five years because it simply did not make sense to continue doing it? Think about people and schools you know that remain prisoners of outmoded, inefficient, or destructive patterns of thinking, routines, and work.

Most organizational change models, including becoming a learning organization, focus primarily on adding new structures and processes to deal with the major problems and challenges. Less well understood, and often times ignored, is the process of leaving behind the old, while adjusting and adopting new perspectives and different ways of accomplishing goals. How is it that organizations, and the people in them, learn to leave behind patterns of thinking, work routines, and outmoded structures and processes while taking on new tools and tasks through organizational learning? The answer is simple: they systematically unlearn or abandon what they currently have and/or know to make room for new ideas and practices that better serve their values, purposes, and goals. Abandonment of outmoded tools and structures, however, does not mean leaving behind deeply held ideals, values, and vision. It simply means pruning nonproductive and negative elements that impede organizational learning and community building.

In my work with teachers and administrators in this country, and in various international settings, I have used the activity of an educational garage sale to help individuals and organizations identify old ideas, routines, structures, and frameworks that no longer fit or work in the organization. Imagine that you were planning an educational garage sale. What would you put out on the driveway? What do the items you have put out for sale reveal about your professional learning and growth in your school? To follow the analogy of the garage sale, remember, there are always buyers for many of these items. When I do this exercise in workshops, the participants' choices about what to get rid of and what is worth keeping evoke rich and thoughtful professional reflections and conversations. The activity also offers an opportunity to build shared understanding, meaning, and professional identity (individual and collective) among participants.

CONCLUSION

In Chapter 1, I described six design themes in the new architecture for professional development. At this point, you will begin to see how each is expressed and combined in unique ways appropriate to create professional learning communities that reflect local culture, goals, and setting. Thus, rather than providing you with a prepackaged, professional development kit—containing all the materials you will need, directions for assembly, and a picture of the model—the new architecture for professional development provides principles, guidelines, tools, and exemplars in practice. Thus, unlike predesigned models that often look out of place and do not quite fit comfortably in the school, your design—grounded in theory, research, and exemplary practice—emerges from local needs and priorities and captures your vision of a professional learning community.

SITE VISITS

www.ncrel.org/sdrs/areas/issues/content/currclum/cu3lk22.htm
North Central Regional Educational Laboratory, Professional Learning Community
www.sedl.org/change/issues/issues61.html
Southwest Educational Development Laboratory
Professional Learning Communities: What Are They and Why Are They Important?
www.nesdec.org/index.html
NESDEC (New England School Development Council) links schools and the research community focused on the development of promising practices. Examples of the latest research focus areas: Special Projects; Professional Learning Communities; Environmental Scanning; and Publications.
www.ethicaledge.com/learning_org.html
Site includes the Ethics of Organizational Learning
www.ascd.org/readingroom/books/wald00book.html
Educators as learners: Creating a professional learning community in your school,
Edited by Penelope J. Wald and Michael S. Castleberry
www.wcer.wisc.edu/step/documents/ola1/ola1.html

Assessing knowledge construction in on-line learning communities, Sharon J. Derry and Lori Adams DuRussel
The Teacher Professional Development Institute employs Internet technology to support distributed professional learning communities.
www.dcvoice.org/professionallearningcomm.html
Professional Learning Communities at Bruce-Monroe Elementary School

SUPPLEMENTARY READINGS

Boyer, E. (1995). *The basic school: A community of learners.* Princeton, NJ: Carnegie Foundation for the Advancement of Teaching.
Collay, M., Dunlap, D., Enloe, W., & Gagnon, G. W. Jr. (1998). *Learning circles: Creating conditions for professional development.* Thousand Oaks, CA: Corwin Press.
Kretzman, J. P., & McKnight, J. L. (1993). *Building communities from inside out: A path toward finding and mobilizing a community asset.* Chicago: ACTA Publications.
Louis, K. S., Kruse, S., & Associates. (1995). *Professionalism and community: Perspectives on reforming urban schools.* Thousand Oaks, CA: Corwin Press.
Sackney, L., & Mitchell, C. (2000). *Profound improvement: Building capacity for a learning community.* Lisse, Netherlands: Swets & Zeitlinger.
Sergiovanni, T. J. (1994). *Building community in schools.* San Francisco: Jossey-Bass.
Sergiovanni, T. J. (1996). *Leadership for the schoolhouse.* San Francisco: Jossey-Bass.
Wenger, E. (1998). *Communities of practice: Learning, meaning, and identity.* Cambridge, UK: Cambridge University Press.

NOTES

1. Kretzman, J. P., & McKnight, J. L. (1993). *Building communities from inside out: A path toward finding and mobilizing a community asset.* Chicago, IL: ACTA Publications.

2. Retrieved July 1, 2002, from www.freedomsnest.com/cgi-bin/qaq.cgi?subject=change&ref=hoferi

3. Mitchell, C., & Sackney, L. (2001). *Building capacity for a learning community.* Paper presented at the International Congress for School Effectiveness and Improvement in Toronto, Canada.

4. Barth, R. (1995). *Building a community of learners.* Oak Brook, IL: NCREL, 3.

5. Collay, M., Dunlap, D., Enloe, W., & Gagnon, G. W. Jr. (1998). *Learning circles: Creating conditions for professional development.* Thousand Oaks, CA: Corwin Press, 3.

6. Sergiovanni, T. J. (1996). *Leadership for the schoolhouse.* San Francisco: Jossey-Bass.

7. Boyer, E. (1995). *The basic school: A community of learners.* Princeton, NJ: Carnegie Foundation for the Advancement of Teaching.

8. Senge, P. (1990). *The fifth discipline: The art and practice of the learning organization*. New York: Currency Doubleday.

9. National Center for Education Statistics. (2000). *Characteristics of the 100 largest public elementary and secondary school districts in the United States: 1998–1999*. Washington, DC: Author. Retrieved July 1, 2002, from http://nces.ed.gov/pubs2001/100largest/highlights.html

10. Senge, P. M. (1990). *The fifth discipline*. New York: Currency Doubleday.

11. See, for example, Greeno, J. G., Collins, A. M., & Resnick, L. B. (1996). Cognition and learning. In D. Berliner & R. Clafee (Eds.), *Handbook of educational psychology*. New York: Simon & Schuster Macmillan; *How people learn: Brain, mind, experience, and school*. Retrieved July 1, 2002 from www.nap.edu

12. Putnam, R. (1995). Bowling alone: America's declining social capital. *Journal of Democracy, 6*(1), 65–78.

13. Wenger, E. (1998). *Communities of practice: Learning, meaning, and identity*. Cambridge, UK: Cambridge University Press.

14. Boyer, E. (1995). *The basic school: A community of learners*. Princeton, NJ: Carnegie Foundation for the Advancement of Teaching.

15. Gardner, J. (1995). Building a responsive community. In A. Etzioni (Ed.), *Rights and the common good: The communitarian perspective*. New York: St. Martin's Press.

16. Meier, D. (1995). How our schools could be. *Phi Delta Kappan, 76*(5): 369–373.

17. Wohlstetter, P., & Griffin, N. (1998). *Creating and sustaining learning communities: Early lessons from charter schools*. CPRE Occasional Paper. University of Pennsylvania: Consortium for Policy Research in Education.

18. Ibid.

19. Mitchell, C., & Sackney, L. (2001). *Building capacity for a learning community*. Paper presented at the International Congress for School Effectiveness and Improvement. Toronto, Canada.

20. Barth, R. (1995). *Building a community of learners*. Oak Brook, IL: NCREL, 3.

21. For a more complete description of these five disciplines the reader should refer to the following texts. Senge, P. (1990). *The fifth discipline: The art and practice of the learning organization*. New York: Currency Doubleday. Senge, P., Kleiner, A., Roberts, C., Ross, R. D., & Smith, B. J. (1994). *The fifth discipline fieldbook*. New York: Doubleday. Senge, P., Kleiner, A., Roberts, C., Ross, R. D., & Smith, B. J. (1999). *The dance of change*. New York: Doubleday

22. See the following resources for descriptions of a PLC survey: Hord, S. M. (1997). Austin, TX: Southwest Educational Development Laboratory; Hord, S. M. (1999). Assessing a school staff as a community of professional learners. *Issues About Change 7*(11); and retrieved July 1, 2002, from www.sedl.org/pubs/catalog/items/cha37.html

Part II

Creating Learning
Spaces In and Beyond
Work

4

Professional Development "As" Work

Staff development is at the center of all educational reform strategies—without it, such strategies are merely good ideas that cannot find expression.[1]

INTRODUCTION

There is an emerging consensus among educational practitioners, researchers, and policy makers that investment in people, through a wide variety of professional development opportunities, is essential to successful educational reform and school improvement initiatives. Research on successful professional development practices provides evidence that the most powerful learning opportunities for teachers and principals are ones embedded in their daily work and linked to the context and priorities of local school improvement efforts.[2] Staff development and inservice training for teachers and principals have been a staple in schools for decades. However, many early release times and scheduled days for staff development have been viewed as add-ons to already busy teacher workdays, or worse, time off for teachers and principals. In this chapter, I argue that the new architecture for professional development represents an expanded view of professional learning and practice. For teachers and principals, professional development is legitimate professional work; it is not time off from work.

EXPANDING THE CONCEPT
OF PROFESSIONAL DEVELOPMENT

I believe it is important to reinforce this message because professional development historically has often been relegated to the status of an educational "stepchild." One prominent scholar offers a grim assessment of teacher professional development, "as generally practiced, has a terrible reputation among scholars, policy makers, and educators alike as being pedagogically unsound, economically inefficient, and of little value to teachers."[3] There are a number of reasons that help explain the litany of problems that have plagued traditional professional development in schools. Staff development and inservice activities are often piecemeal, fragmented, and incoherent in their design and delivery. Often these activities are only tangentially connected to teachers' and principals' everyday work needs and demands. In some instances, the focus of the training is limited to important technical skills but ones that fail to deal with the complexities and demands of classroom teaching and school leadership. Other criticisms include the lack of connection between ongoing professional learning and preservice preparation and socialization; the lack of a developmental focus that differentiates the knowledge, needs, and skills of novices and experts; and the general lack of follow-up resources and support to sustain favorable conditions for professional learning and change.[4] As a result, when budgets are tight, with the acquiescence of school board members and practitioners, monies for staff and professional development often become easy targets for balancing the books. Poorly designed and delivered inservices and workshops also have engendered cynicism and provoked educators to think of these training sessions more as exercises in organizational compliance than in professional growth.

Rethinking Professional Development: New State Regulations

Being committed to advancing one's learning and expanding one's professional knowledge and expertise are hallmarks of what it means to be a professional. Thus, the very nature of educators' professional work is anchored in ongoing learning that strengthens expertise and practice, contributing to student achievement and organizational improvement. New state licensing standards for teachers and principals, as well as redesigned teacher evaluation processes in schools, reinforce the importance of professional development and expert practice.[5] For example, in Wisconsin all new teachers and principals begin their professional work under a five-year, nonrenewable license granted after completion of preparation programs with specific performance-based standards for professional practice. In addition to the performance-based framework that guides licensing requirements, a major change comes in the renewal of professional licenses. Over a five-year period all teachers and principals are required to design, implement, and document an individual professional development plan that will be the basis of their application for license renewal. The new regulations also require each licensee to work with mentors, local school administrators, and faculty in colleges and universities across the state. The new licensing system was designed to do away with unproductive activities masquerading as professional development including the accumulations of credits on any topic, taken in any sequence, with no regard for the connections among individual professional needs, school improvement goals, and student learning outcomes. Documentation of enhanced professional knowledge and performance in an individual professional development plan is required for the license renewal and advancement.

Professional Development and Teacher Evaluation

Teacher evaluation processes in schools also hold the potential for transforming teacher learning and professional development. Formative evaluation frameworks, such as ones designed by Charlotte Danielson and Thomas L. McGreal, and Allan A. Glatthorn and Linda E. Fox link ongoing professional growth and learning to high-quality professional practice.[6] A framework that simultaneously ensures quality professional performance while supporting and promoting individual growth creates tension in terms of traditional roles, relationships, and responsibilities among educational professionals. The go-it-alone, survivalist view of the beginning teacher is replaced by a new set of professional relationships between teachers and supervisors. In evaluation processes that emphasize growth and improvement more than summative judgments, supervisors focus on learning and enhanced practice, not perfection. The teacher is free to be vulnerable and risk discussing his or her limitations, concerns, and lack of experience that affect work with students and colleagues. Building new professional relationships creates a professional learning environment that is characterized more by support than summative judgment, more by encouragement than numeric ratings, and more by trust than teacher trial and error.

THE NATURE AND CONTEXT
OF PROFESSIONAL WORK IN SCHOOLS

We have a rich literature on teaching as work. This body of work includes vivid historic accounts of teaching in small rural schools, classic sociological studies, such as those by Willard Waller and Dan Lortie,[7] and richly detailed ethnographic descriptions.[8] There is a similar body of literature that describes the work of school principals. Among other things, we know principals' workdays consist of hundreds of verbal and interpersonal interactions that require high levels of energy and multitask capabilities; frequent interruptions; a complex mix of varied, brief, and oftentimes unexpected tasks; and rewards that come primarily from the successes of others (students and staff).[9]

These works, and many others, provide a narrative backdrop for understanding professional development within the context of everyday professional work in schools—revealing conditions that support or impede adult learning, the dilemmas and contradictions that create tension for practitioners, and the rhythms and regularities of life and work in schools. How does the nature of teachers' and principals' daily work in schools influence professional learning and growth?

Characteristics of Professional Work in Schools

A review of the literature on the sociology of teachers' work suggests six common features that I will use to illustrate the relationship between the nature and context of professional work in schools and professional learning. My list is a selective one, not meant to capture all features of professional work in schools. Common characteristics include (a) uncertainties in teaching and leading; (b) norms of privacy and individualism; (c) paradoxes in practice; (d) the importance of psychic rewards; (e) personalized practice; and (f) "the grammar of schooling."[10] Each has important implications for the design, delivery, and outcomes of professional development.

Uncertainties in Teaching and Leading. A major theme in the literature on teacher and principal work is that it is fraught with uncertainties. The complex nature of teaching, learning, and leadership in schools makes the idea of a professional knowledge base that provides ready solutions and easy answers to such perennial problems as lack of motivation, truancy, school dropouts, and poor achievement problematic. There is a substantial body of literature that informs good professional practice. We know a good deal about teaching and learning. However, when applied in practice this knowledge base is conditional and situational in that it provides a repertoire of possibilities for effective teaching and learning strategies and does not provide a menu of right answers to problems of practice. Experienced educators know that what works well with one student or one class at one time will not necessarily have the same result in the future. Thus, even the most knowledgeable and experienced educators are ready to shift strategies and use very different methods than originally planned when confronted with unexpected conditions or outcomes.

As a result, teachers and principals tend to rely more on their personal and collective experiences than on research to guide their practice. Because of the fast pace and challenging aspects of professional work in schools, teachers and principals have preferences for information and ideas that they can put into practice immediately—ones that are amenable to adaptation and personal teaching and leadership styles.[11] Educators are inveterate "tinkerers" who modify and personalize ideas and methods that fit their own preferences, routines, settings, and students' needs. For example, imagine a department of high school English teachers all committed to implementing a newly revised, standards-based curriculum. Notwithstanding the collaborative thinking and work that went into the new curriculum, it is only a guide in the hands of veteran teachers. The course description listed in the student handbook suggests that English 10 is English 10 is English 10 regardless of who teaches the class. Experienced educators know that the ambiguities of teaching anchored in the mix of diverse student needs, teacher expertise and experiences, and the dynamic interplay of teacher and students will result in a wide range of English 10 learning activities and experiences. This is not a weakness in the curriculum or in organizational structure. It is simply one of the realities of teaching and learning.

Norms of Privacy and Individualism. Although there are notable examples to suggest that teachers and principals are beginning to establish collaborative work settings,[12] powerful norms of privacy and individualism continue to characterize professional work in schools. In part, these norms are a legacy of one-room schools where teachers historically worked in isolation from other adults, learned to be self-sufficient, and developed highly personalized styles for teaching. Though housed in the same building, many teachers and principals who work side-by-side physically still maintain their professional and psychological privacy in self-contained classrooms and offices. Clearly these norms vary from school to school and across levels—elementary through high school. What is important is to recognize how norms of privacy and individualism influence professional development opportunities. Because work settings are such rich places for professional learning, norms of privacy and individualism limit growth and development opportunities in school. For instance, they frustrate teachers' and principals' attempts to share professional knowledge systematically; carry out joint work and learning; conduct collaborative inquiry; promote team learning; and design organizational improvement efforts around shared goals and purposes.

Paradoxes in Practice. The work of teachers and principals is also characterized by some fundamental contradictions creating professional tension and uncertainty. For example, every teacher and principal knows that each child is unique, brings different strengths and experiences to school, and has individual needs. However, because educators generally work with students in groups, rather than with just one student at a time, there is a natural tension between meeting each child's needs and being able to accomplish work simultaneously with a group of 25 to 30 energetic students. Working with groups requires a variety of control mechanisms (organizational structures, rules, discipline policies) to help educators deal effectively with the daily realities of their work.

Another paradox in professional work is grounded in *routine* versus *renewal.* On the one hand, in order to be successful in their work, teachers and principals must develop highly skilled and routinized strategies for dealing with a complex array of teaching and learning challenges. Yet the very routines necessary for successful practice may limit or impede further professional growth and development. Because various habits of mind and action are so deeply embedded in professional work, they are often difficult to unlearn or abandon even when new ideas and methods may be more promising. The implication for professional development and change is obvious. Significant time, practice, and support are needed to help teachers and principals to abandon old practices while they develop professional comfort and control with newly learned knowledge and skills.

A third contradictory force affecting teachers and principals is the tension between professional autonomy and measures of accountability. As professionals, teachers and principals have advanced training, knowledge, and expertise. Based on this level of qualification, they are hired to work for the best interests of their students. However, educator professional autonomy is constrained by demands for accountability that supervisors, local school boards, and various policy and political agencies impose on their work. The issue is not whether teachers and principals should be accountable—of course, they should be! The real issue is what are the most appropriate mechanisms for making judgments about their performance and its impact on student learning and development? Examples of the tension between professional autonomy and accountability abound in current debates and decisions concerning such topics as academic standards, student testing, and performance evaluation.

What are some ways the tension that exists between autonomy and accountability affects professional learning? First, newly promulgated academic standards and testing requirements of students, often unrelated to local school improvement plans and priorities, have consumed resources (time, personnel, and dollars) for professional development and compliance. As a result, fewer resources remain to support individual or local professional development priorities. The fact that governing bodies believe they have greater insight into individual professional learning needs and priorities is itself a major limitation to professional learning. Policy makers have a legitimate interest in investments made to enhance professional practice and student learning outcomes. That interest, however, should not disregard teachers' and principals' professional autonomy and responsibility for updating and enhancing their practice. In a recent report, *Teachers Take Charge of Their Learning*, published by the National Foundation of the Improvement of Education, the authors present a compelling rationale for educators to assume control and responsibility for their ongoing professional development.[13]

Importance of Psychic Rewards. Given the highly personalized nature of teaching and learning, it should come as no surprise that teachers' and principals' primary rewards and satisfactions come from working with students and staff.[14] Working with students, being able to positively influence their development, and helping them learn are among the factors that attract people to careers in education and keep them there. Extrinsic rewards—salary, working conditions, and benefit—are important, but they are not the primary incentives that influence educators. Knowing what motivates teachers and principals, as well as identifying sources of dissatisfaction, is important to professional development planning and implementation. Being able to work with students and student learning are primary motivators for teachers. Thus, professional development opportunities that link professional practices to students and their learning outcomes are much more likely to engage busy educators. Current research indicates that the most effective professional development focuses on student learning, helps teachers and principals examine differences between desired and actual student learning outcomes, is grounded in the analysis and interpretation of student learning outcome data, and is connected to a coherent and comprehensive framework for improved student learning.[15]

Personalized Professional Practice. To address the mix of complexity, paradox, and policy, teachers and administrators tend to develop highly personalized styles in their work. And, because the rewards of their works are anchored in the successes of others—that is, students and staff—the relationships they develop with others is a major factor influencing their success. While there are aspects of teaching and school leadership that lend themselves to established programs, rationality, and uses of technology, much of what these educational professionals rely on daily is a creative blend of knowledge, skills, values, commitments, and personal qualities. Like artists, highly effective teachers and principals manage to combine experience, knowledge, and technique in imaginative ways to match personal capacities to the demands of their work. What are the implications for professional development? Gone is the idea that one activity or program serves the needs of everyone. Like all learners, teachers and principals bring different experiences, prior knowledge, and needs to various learning opportunities. In addition, new ideas and change in practice often bring cognitive dissonance and conflict. Professionals need time, resources, and support to help them adjust to and integrate new ideas, technology, and behaviors to levels of routine practice.

The Grammar of Schooling.[16] The enduring features of schools and schooling in the United States also have a profound influence on professional development. Notwithstanding decades of educational reform initiatives, these features persist in schools and affect all aspects of education. For instance, age and grade levels are the dominant organizational structure in schools today. In heavily urbanized and surburbanized school districts, school calendars continue to reflect planting and harvesting rhythms of America in the 19th and early 20th century. Many of these features are so deeply ingrained in our notion of schooling that we often do not even question why they continue to exist. Because schooling is a common experience, we each have an image of what a *real* school is. Even when educational reform initiatives are well designed and will serve identified needs, significant changes in culture, process, and structure that run counter to our mental images of school face strong resistance. I refer to the tension between the opposing forces of school change and its grammar as *dynamic sameness*: There is pressure to change education to meet new realities, but whatever we create must conform to our mental image of what a *real* school is.

The grammar of schooling affects both the nature of work and professional development in schools. Perhaps the best way to illustrate the connections between an enduring structural feature of schools and professional work and learning is to pose some questions. For instance, as an experienced educator, do you see important differences between the way(s) in which high school, middle school, and elementary teachers define and carry out their work? How might grade levels influence the way(s) in which teachers and principals think about student learning and growth? about curriculum content and design? about teaching methods? Does the notion of grade level influence the way teachers think about their own professional learning and growth? How might the grade level organization of a school impede the creation of a professional learning community?

Bringing vertically organized grade-level teams together to work on curriculum or districtwide issues, for instance, provides another opportunity to observe the relationship between the grammar of schooling and professional work and learning. At first, the exchanges among elementary, middle, and high school teachers often seem awkward—some teachers wonder what they can possibly talk about given the differences in their professional assignments. As members of the team begin to describe their commitments, passions, and views on content, teaching, and students, the structural and cultural barriers of grade levels give way to new insights and understandings among professional colleagues. Joint work and team learning represent a type of professional development activity that forges shared purpose, reinforces mutual commitments, and strengthens collective organizational capacity.

TOWARD A NEW ARCHITECTURE
FOR PROFESSIONAL DEVELOPMENT:
THREE MAJOR SHIFTS

More than a decade ago, Susan Rosenholtz made a distinction between two general types of schools: *Learning-enriched schools* were ones characterized

Figure 4.1 Toward a New Architecture for Professional Development: Conceptual Shifts

Traditional Professional Development		New Architecture for Professional Development
From	$\rightarrow$	*To*
Add-on, frill, educational stepchild	$\rightarrow$	Professional development as essential work
Individualized learning	$\rightarrow$	Collaborative learning and growth
Activity centered	$\rightarrow$	Linked to practice and student learning
Before, after, and outside of work	$\rightarrow$	Embedded in daily work
Emphasis on outside ideas and expertise	$\rightarrow$	Internal capacity for improvement
Focus on individual learning and change	$\rightarrow$	Focus on collective expertise and practice

by norms of ongoing professional learning, collaboration, and innovation; *Learning-impoverished schools* were sterile and negative workplaces that limited teacher development and school improvement.[17] Moving from learning-impoverished to learning-enriched professional work environments requires significant changes in schools and the nature of the professional work in them.

Figures 4.1, 4.2, and 4.3 illustrate three major shifts—conceptual, structural, and cultural—necessary to move toward a new architecture for professional development in schools. Why are these major shifts needed? Dramatic shifts in each of these areas are needed in order to move professional development from the margins of educators' work experiences—that is, scheduled before and after busy school days, as well as periodically sprinkled throughout the academic year—to the core of daily professional work responsibilities. The first is a *conceptual shift* that describes important changes in the way(s) educators and educational stakeholders think about professional development and its link to teaching and learning in schools. The second is a *structural shift* in schools and communities, one that fosters the creative use of resources and organizational structures to redesign organizational structures and process to support the creation and maintenance of a true professional learning community in schools. The third is a *cultural shift* reflecting major changes in values, norms, and practices that reveal the essence of a professional learning community. In each of the figures, the column on the left lists various conditions and factors in traditional, oftentimes learning-impoverished schools, that limit opportunities for professional development as work. The column on the right represents the characteristics of, and conditions that support, professional learning communities.

Conceptual Shifts

The ways in which educators, parents, and policy makers think and talk about professional development tell us a great deal about the status and nature of professional learning in the community. I use a recent newspaper editorial to illustrate my point.[18] In this piece, the local editors have taken a stand on the issue of whether local school districts or the state legislature should determine the starting date for schools. Their position statement is laced with negative language revealing a true disdain for the importance of professional development in education. "There remain, however, those pesky half-days: 11 in the Monona district. These are teacher inservice days, or time off teaching to prepare report cards." It seems to these journalists that providing opportunities for professional development is a "pesky" problem and is "time off teaching" where teachers are likely to spend time doing seemingly unimportant work—evaluating the learning of their students. Unfortunately, this language, and the thinking that goes with it, is not unique. They represent old stereotypes and the adverse conditions that characterize learning impoverished traditional schools and communities.

Figure 4.1 identifies six notable conceptual differences between traditional schools and ones characterized as professional learning communities. In a learning-enriched school community, professional learning and growth are:

- Essential to work, not marginal tasks or time off "real work."
- Collaborative with shared purpose, not solitary activities.
- Developmentally appropriate and linked to student-school-teacher priorities, not fragmented unaligned events.
- Embedded in daily work, not something other than work.
- Centered in expertise and capacity building within, not solely dependent on ideas and models from outside the school.
- Focused on enhancing collective professional knowledge and capacity, not just individual learning.

The intensity and magnitude of these conceptual shifts will vary dramatically across schools and districts. The degree to which a school reflects the characteristics in the right-hand column indicates that it is moving positively toward becoming a professional learning community.

Structural Shifts

The new architecture for professional development also reveals a number of structural differences from traditional schools. There are at least seven key areas where changes in organizational structures and processes help move schools in the direction of becoming professional learning communities (see Figure 4.2). First, the design and delivery of professional

Figure 4.2 Toward a New Architecture for Professional Development: Structural Shifts

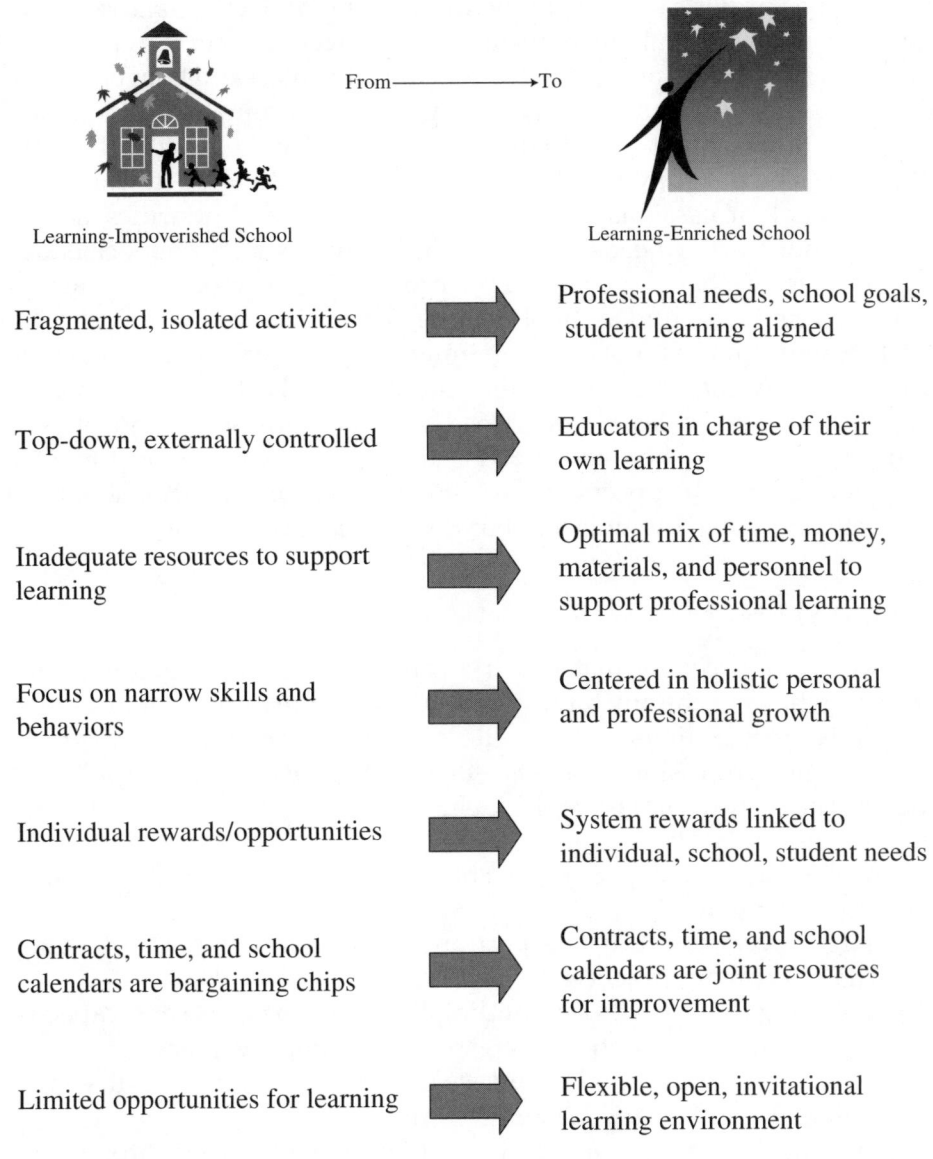

development in a professional learning community is continuous and fully aligned with student learning and organizational improvement goals. Professional development is not fragmented and incoherent. Second, rather than hierarchically imposed staff development programs and events, teachers and principals assume responsibility for and control of their own learning. In professional learning communities, decisions on professional development content, delivery, resources, and evaluations are made by those closest to and most affected by those decisions—teachers and principals. Third, unlike impoverished school settings where resources are often inadequate and inconsistent, professional learning communities provide sufficient time for learning, reflection, and consultation. There is an optimal mix of materials, resources, and support personnel who are willing, able, and available to support professional development. Fourth, teacher evaluation focuses on growth, continuous learning, and improved practice, not on infrequent, narrow summative ratings of pre-defined teaching behaviors. Fifth, system and individual rewards and incentives link professional learning to school goals and priorities, not just to individual teacher needs. Sixth, teacher contracts and school calendars are products of shared purpose and professional responsibility among teachers, administrators, school boards, and local communities. Staff development time is not a bargaining chip in win-lose adversarial bargaining between teachers and the school board. Last, the seventh structural shift evident in learning-enriched schools is the social and physical architecture. Rather than privatized learning spaces that tend to isolate professionals from their peers, the new architecture for professional learning is flexible and open, inviting collaborative work and learning.

Cultural Shifts

If you visit a school that is a true professional learning community, before you have spent much time there you begin to notice important features of its organizational culture—its expression of core values, norms of practice, and professional beliefs—that distinguish it from traditional schools. The features in Figure 4.3 include:

- Colleague interdependence, shared knowledge, and openness to improvement.
- High levels of mutual respect and trust that support professional dialogue about practice.
- Learning that focuses on building collective expertise and capacity.
- An emphasis on continuous learning and improvement.
- Conversation, symbols, and ceremonies demonstrate that they value, recognize, and celebrate learning.
- A "can do" spirit anchored in high personal and professional efficacy.

The positive aspects of school culture listed above stand out because they are in such stark contrast to features in learning-impoverished school settings. These have been described as "potholes of pestilence," that result from weak leadership and official neglect. "The buildings, dirty and in dis-repair, are unwholesome environments for learning and child growth. The schools are poorly staffed and equipped. The morale of teachers and pupils

Figure 4.3   Toward a New Architecture for Professional Development: Cultural Shifts

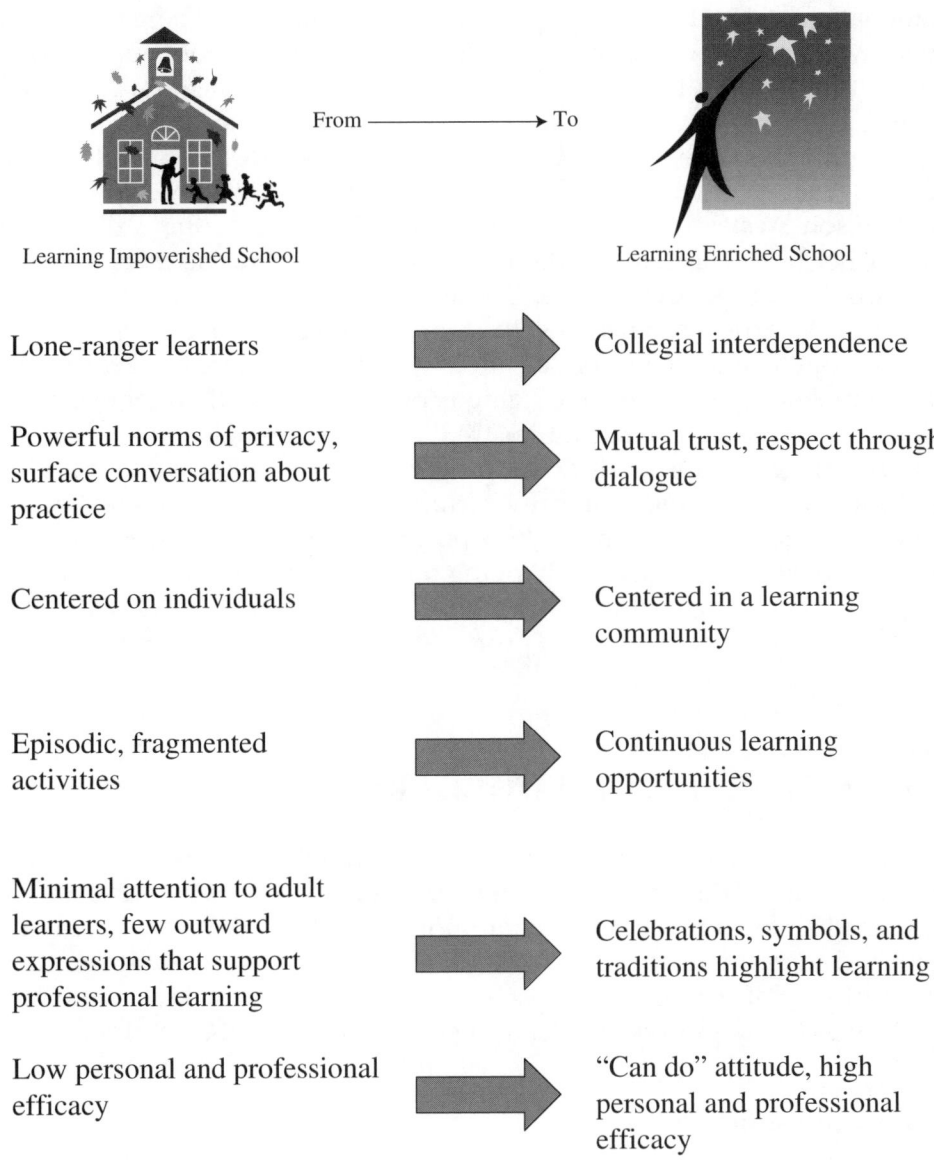

From ——————→ To

Learning Impoverished School   Learning Enriched School

Lone-ranger learners ——————→ Collegial interdependence

Powerful norms of privacy, surface conversation about practice ——————→ Mutual trust, respect through dialogue

Centered on individuals ——————→ Centered in a learning community

Episodic, fragmented activities ——————→ Continuous learning opportunities

Minimal attention to adult learners, few outward expressions that support professional learning ——————→ Celebrations, symbols, and traditions highlight learning

Low personal and professional efficacy ——————→ "Can do" attitude, high personal and professional efficacy

is low; where control is maintained, fear is one of the essential strategies employed. Instructional programs are traditional, ritualistic, and poorly related to student needs. The schools are characterized by unenthusiasm, squalor, and ineffectiveness."[19] Impoverished school learning environments negatively affect everyone in schools, perhaps most dramatically the children. Sadly, and nearly a half century later, Jonathan Kozol described in vivid detail the impact of impoverished schools on children. "Bleakness was the order of the day in fifth grade science. The children were studying plant biology when I came in, but not with lab equipment. There was none. There was a single sink that may have worked but was not being used, a couple of test tubes locked up in a cupboard, and a skeleton also locked behind glass windows. The nearly total blankness of the walls was interrupted only by a fire safety poster. The window shades were badly torn. The only textbook I could find (*Mathematics in Our World*) had been published by Addison-Wesley in 1973. A chart of 'The Elements' on the wall behind the teacher listed no elements discovered in the past four decades."[20]

I think you get the picture. These are stifling school environments where professional practice is solitary and privatized; norms of privacy prevent open and deep conversation about professional practice and shared purpose; professional learning is primarily an individual responsibility; more emphasis is placed on credits and credentials than on collective learning; professional development is an activity, not a part of professional work; and, cynically, dispirited faculty offer more "yeah-buts" and "reasons why not" than positive responses to new learning opportunities and initiatives. Changing these negative aspects of learning-impoverished school cultures is a daunting challenge; it is, nonetheless, fundamental to the creation of a professional learning community.

IMPLICATIONS FOR EDUCATIONAL STAKEHOLDERS

Professional development "as" work has a number of implications for teachers, administrators, and school boards. Efforts to create and sustain a successful and healthy learning community over time require the commitment and coordination of efforts by each of these major stakeholder groups. I present a set of challenges for teachers, administrators, and school boards working to create professional learning communities in their districts.

Implications for Teachers

If you are a teacher:

1. The next time someone says, or even suggests, that inservice and professional development days for teachers are time off, or worse yet, "vacation days," speak up! Tell others why professional development is important to you.

2. As a professional, you are responsible for your professional growth and improved practice. Convenience, credits, and credentials should not determine your professional learning.

3. As you plan your professional learning, you should be able to articulate and document the connections between your professional development activities and student learning/school goals.

4. As you begin to deprivatize your teaching practice and professional learning, you will experience both its risks and rewards.

5. Creating a learning-enriched school culture means abandoning any tendencies of individual ownership of professional knowledge, practice, materials, and space.

6. As a member of a collective teaching and learning community, you need to develop a capacity for dialogue centered on student learning and professional practice.

7. Because resources in any organization are limited, you will work with colleagues to develop criteria and processes for allocating scarce resources to support learning priorities for individuals and groups.

8. Last, individually and collectively, you need to evaluate professional development at multiple levels to determine its impact.

Implications for Administrators

Leaders have a substantial influence on professional development. The following are implications of the new architecture for professional development for school administrators.

School leaders should:

- Avoid being a gatekeeper for teachers' professional development. Principals and other administrators need to help teachers articulate and take responsibility for their own professional learning and improved practice.
- Be positive advocates for professional development in and beyond the school.
- Make professional development an essential component for teacher evaluation.
- Work with teachers, school boards members, and other administrators to develop criteria, structures, and processes for allocating resources to support professional development.
- Avoid hijacking times and resources set aside for professional development to complete administrative work or organizational maintenance activities.
- Demonstrate the importance of professional learning and high-quality practice by being a model learner, one who participates and supports learning opportunities, and recognizes the importance of professional development in school.

- Provide appropriate and adequate resources (time, money, personnel, and materials) to support professional learning and improved practice.
- Use creative tension to challenge, stimulate, and energize colleagues strengthening their reflective capacities and deepening their commitment to high-quality professional practice.
- Provide support—expertise, psychological and emotional comfort—to help teachers deal with some of the challenges, discomforts, and dissonance that accompany new learning, strategic abandonment, and adjustments to practice.

Implications for School Boards

School board members are the formal links between the local community and the district's professional staff. Their understanding and support for professional development for teachers and administration are vital to maintaining high levels of professional commitment and practice in the district and to meeting overall district educational goals. School board members need to:

- Make professional development an essential component of employee formative and summative evaluations.
- Resist the temptation to see professional development resources as easy items to cut when budget reductions are necessary.
- Provide adequate resources to support enriched school learning communities.
- Evaluate professional development activities, investments, and outcomes.
- Articulate in local policies and public deliberations the importance of high-quality professional development to school/district educational goals.
- Be willing to experiment with such structures as time, calendar, contract language, and organization processes to create optimal conditions and opportunities for professional learning "in," "at," and "beyond" the district.
- Recognize, reward, and celebrate professional learning and its outcomes—for teachers, administrators, students, schools, and the community.
- Include professional development as a fundamental component in strategic planning processes.

CONCLUSION

Professional development "as" work is a prominent feature of the new architecture for professional development. Moving professional development from the margins of professional work to its core requires major shifts—conceptual shifts, structural shifts, and shifts in the professional learning cultures of schools. Professional development as work presents significant challenges as well as promising opportunities for teachers, school administrators, and school boards working to create a new architecture for professional development in education.

SITE VISITS

www.nea.org/helpfrom
National Educational Helpfrom is a place designed to assist adults workings with students.
www.nhc.rtp.nc.us/tserve/tserve.htm
TeacherServe from the National Humanities Center is an interactive curriculum enrichment service for teachers.
www.teachers.net
A great resource for teachers offering everything from chat boards to lesson ideas.

SUPPLEMENTARY READING

Danielson, C., & McGreal, T. L. (2000). Teacher evaluation to enhance professional practice. Alexandria, VA: Association for Supervision and Curriculum Development.

Moore Johnson, S. (1990). *Teachers at work: Achieving success in our schools.* New York: Basic Books.

National Foundation for the Improvement of Education (NFIE). (1996). *Teachers take charge of their learning.* Washington, DC: Author.

Rosenholtz, S. (1989). *Teachers' workplace: The social organization of schools.* New York: Longman.

NOTES

1. Sparks, D., & Hirsch, S. (1997). *A new vision for staff development.* Alexandria, VA: Association for Supervision and Curriculum Development, 96.

2. Smylie, M. A. (1996). From bureaucratic control to building human capital: The importance of teacher learning in education reform. *Educational Researcher, 25*(9), 9–11.

3. Ibid.

4. Bredeson, P. V. (1999). *Paradox and possibility: Professional development and organizational learning in education.* Paper presented at the American Educational Research Conference in Montreal, Canada.

5. Wisconsin Department of Public Instruction (2000). Teacher Education and Licensing, PI 34. Retrieved July 1, 2002, from www.dpi.state.wi.us

6. Danielson, C., & McGreal T. L. (2000). *Teacher evaluation to enhance professional practice.* Alexandria, VA: Association for Supervision and Curriculum Development; Glatthorn, A. A., & Fox, L. E. (1996). *Quality teaching through professional development.* Thousand Oaks, CA: Corwin Press

7. Waller, W. (1932) *The sociology of teaching.* New York: Wiley; Lortie, D. (1975). *Schoolteacher.* Chicago: University of Chicago Press.

8. See for example: Rosenholtz, S. (1989) *Teachers' workplace*: *The social organization of schools.* New York: Longman; Moore Johnson, S. (1990) *Teachers at work: Achieving success in our schools.* New York: Basic Books; Metz, M. H. (1978*). Classrooms and corridors: The crisis of authority in desegregated secondary schools.* Berkeley: University of California Press.

9. For example, the works of Wolcott, H. F. (1973). *The man in the principal's office: An ethnography.* New York: Holt, Rinehart, & Winston. Hart, A. W., & Bredeson, P. V. (1996). *The principalship: A theory of professional learning and practice.* New York: McGraw-Hill. Reitzug, U.C., & Reeves, J. E. (1992). Miss Lincoln doesn't teach here: A descriptive narrative and conceptual analysis of a principal's symbolic leadership behavior. *Educational Administration Quarterly 29*(2), 185–219.

10. Tyack, D., & Tobin, W. (1994). The "grammar" of schooling: Why has it been so hard to change? *American Educational Research Journal, 31*(3), 453–479.

11. Bredeson, P. V., & Scribner, J. P. (2000). A statewide professional development conference: Useful strategy for learning or inefficient use of resources? Retrieved July 1, 2002, from http://epaa.asu.edu/epaa/v8n13/

12. Louis, K. S., Kruse, S., & Associates (1995). *Professionalism and community: Perspectives on reforming urban schools.* Thousand Oaks, CA: Corwin Press.

13. *Teachers take charge of their learning* (1996). National Foundation for the Improvement of Education (NFIE). Washington, DC:

14. Bredeson, P. V., Kasten, K. L., & Fruth, M. J. (1983). Rewards and incentives in secondary school teaching. *Journal of Research and Development in Education.*

15. *Improving professional development: Eight research based principles.* National Partnership for Excellence and Accountability. Retrieved July 1, 2002, from http://www.npeat.org

16. Tyack, D., & Tobin, W. (1994). The "grammar" of schooling: Why has it been so hard to change? *American Educational Research Journal, 31*(3), 453–479.

17. Rosenholtz, S. (1989). *Teachers' workplace.* New York: Longman.

18. Parents like starting school in September, *Wisconsin State Journal,* August 24, 2001, A10.

19. Becker, G., Withycombe, R., Doyel, F., Miller, E., Morgan, C., DeLoretto, L., Aldridge, B., & Goldhammer,. K. (1971). *Elementary school principals and their schools: Beacons of brilliance and potholes of pestilence.* Eugene, OR: Center for the Advanced Study of Educational Administration, 2.

20. Kozol, J. (1991). *Savage inequalities: Children in America's schools.* New York: Crown.

5

Professional Development *"In"* Work

There has been increasing recognition that teachers and teachers' knowledge gained from and embedded in their everyday work with children should be at the center of reform efforts and professional development activities.[1]

INTRODUCTION

Recently, a school superintendent was asked, "During the school day, what opportunities do teachers have to get better at teaching?" Her response captures the major theme for this chapter.

> Now, that's a loaded question! It's a strange question. I would hope that by their very act of working with children, if they are doing real action research and paying attention to the student work, they're learning. And that's one of the best things that should be happening for their professional development. Sending them off to a conference is probably about fourth down on the list. The number one happens right here in the classroom every day. Maybe number two and number three are probably some shared planning times, but number one is in the classroom with kids if they understand and if they are really focused on student learning, and know how

to assess, and know what results to look for in terms of how students are improving.[2]

In this chapter, we examine learning opportunities embedded in the daily work of teachers and principals. I begin with a definition of *professional development in work*. Next is a discussion of what we know from research and effective practice that supports job-embedded learning. In the third section, I present various opportunities for professional learning embedded in teachers' work in schools. The following section contains a discussion of professional development "in" work. This section also describes motivators and barriers to job-embedded professional development in schools. The chapter concludes with an assessment of professional development in work against the three criteria underlying the definition of professional development.

DEFINING PROFESSIONAL DEVELOPMENT "IN" WORK

Professional development "in" work refers to a rich variety of learning opportunities embedded in a person's daily work. For teachers and principals, this means a constellation of work activities and responsibilities. In the literature, such terms as "job-embedded learning," "on-the-job learning," and "informal learning at work" are commonly used. I use the concept of *professional development "in" work,* because it describes more than individual learning in the workplace. It links individual learning, growth, and development to organizational purpose, communities of practice, and collective capacity. Because educators' work is intense, complex, and varied, venues for professional learning embedded in daily work routines are numerous. Notwithstanding the variety and abundance of these opportunities, most are constrained by the demands and dilemmas that characterize teaching and school leadership. I use the term professional development "in" work to distinguish it from professional development "at" work (on-site or workplace learning), which I describe in Chapter 6.

What do we mean when we use the concept of teaching as work?[3] In some cases, we are simply referring to teaching as an *occupation*, one that distinguishes it from engineering, dentistry, or law. Another view is the *enterprise of teaching*—all of the tasks and activities that accompany and support teaching. This includes such things as planning for instruction, preparing materials, taking attendance, completing required paperwork, supervising students at events, and communicating with parents, to name a few. The *act of teaching* includes all the things teachers say and do when they are working directly with students, including supportive and intellectual acts. Prompting, reinforcing, drilling, and stimulating interest among students are examples of supportive teaching acts. Teaching is also an intellectual act. The core of teaching is helping students use their minds to become aware of particular ideas, to understand something, and/or to develop specific skills and knowledge. In this chapter teaching as work includes the *enterprise* behaviors of teaching as well as the *acts* of teaching. I will describe a broad range of professional learning opportunities embedded in teachers' daily activities and professional responsibilities.

JOB-EMBEDDED LEARNING: SOME THINGS WE KNOW

Personal work experience, research on job-embedded learning, and literature in the area of adult cognition provide ample support for professional development "in" work. Let us review some things we know about job-embedded learning and on-the-job learning opportunities for teachers and principals. We know the following:

- Most on-the-job learning tends to be informal, varied, and multifaceted. "Informal learning (everyday learning) is the most important setting for continuous learning. This form of learning/instruction must be made visible."[4]
- The content of professional development "in" work is inherent in teachers' daily work and is embedded in the context of that work—including the uncertainty, daily rhythms, noise, and personal interactions that characterize teaching.
- Professional development "in" work allows teachers and principals to create shared meaning, build collective capacity, and strengthen norms of communities of practice. "Community is the joining of practice with analysis and reflection to share the tacit understandings and to create shared knowledge from the experiences among participants in a learning opportunity."[5]
- Unlike traditional staff development activities in the workplace or off-site training sessions, professional development that is embedded in teachers' daily work reduces problems associated with transfer of learning.
- Professional development "in" work taps into the characteristics and natural inclinations of adult learners. For example, the literature on adult learning indicates that adults are autonomous and self-directed learners. Adult learners want to connect new learning to their accumulated stock of knowledge and experience. Adult learners prefer learning opportunities that are relevant and have practical applications and benefits. Adult learners are goal-oriented, often linking the content and learning outcomes to particular career goals and work demands.[6]
- Professional development "in" work empowers teachers and principals as learners; they are responsible for their own learning. Grounding aspects of professional learning in teachers' daily work

also legitimizes practical knowledge. Oftentimes, teachers' and principals' personal knowledge and experiences have been treated as less important than theoretical or university-based research knowledge. The ideas, knowledge, and expertise to support professional growth and school improvement are often already within the school, not "out there" or "up there," or in some other place in the educational hierarchy.

- Like all learners, adult learners have different learning styles. Professional development "in" work links learning styles to opportunities for professional learning and growth.
- Much of what teachers do involves interaction with other people, students and adults. Thus, professional development "in" work provides multiple opportunities to reduce isolated individual learning while building social support and connections.
- Teachers and principals continually learn through action and reflection. "Through countless acts of attention and inattention, naming, sensemaking, boundary setting, and control," they have interactive transactions between professional knowing, doing, and learning.[7]

The characteristics of job-embedded learning offer many advantages for teachers' and principals' professional development. Next, we examine the advantages of professional development "in" work.

ADVANTAGES TO PROFESSIONAL DEVELOPMENT "IN" WORK

Given the extensive body of knowledge on job-embedded learning, professional development "in" work has a number of important advantages when compared to other training and development activities. To begin, teachers' and principals' work is continuous and ongoing, so too are the opportunities for professional learning in schools. Despite already busy days with little perceived time left for professional learning, one teacher recently captured the essence of taking advantages of multiple opportunities to learn while working. Here is how that teacher described it:

> Well, there's always time for self-evaluation. I mean every teacher at the end of a lesson has either gone, "Yes, that was awesome!" or, "Oh my God, that totally stunk!" And again, there's that discussion/communication with other people whether you're learning about something they did or getting the chance to critique yourself with somebody else. I end up with a lot of parent volunteers in my room. You know, again, just discussing it makes you think about why I am doing it. You have to be able to explain it to somebody else, then you've got to put some thought into it.[8]

Figure 5.1 Professional Development "In" Work

Learner Activity	Structure of Learning Activity	
	Informal	*Structured*
Individual	Reflection in practice Individual reading	Action research School self-study
Collaborative	Daily interactions Sharing information/ideas	Team teaching Peer coaching

Another major advantage is the close link between professional development content, context, and learning outcomes. Reflection, analysis, and interpretation "in" and "on" teaching are ideally situated and highly relevant. This suggests another advantage—increased motivation. Connecting teaching to professional reflection and growth has practicality, relevance, and applicability; all are important reasons why informal learning motivates teachers. Finally, there are also a number of efficiencies that accompany job-embedded learning. When compared to other traditional forms of professional development—conferences, workshops, and outside consultants—on-the-job learning that taps into collective knowledge and on-site experiences eliminates such costs as travel expenses, salary for substitute teachers, and consulting fees.

PROFESSIONAL LEARNING "IN" WORK

Lack of time is one of the most frequently cited problems that plagues professional development in schools. "When asked about their need for planning time, learning time, and group decision-making time, teachers are clear that it cannot be found within the current school schedule or by reducing time with students."[9] To address this problem, many school districts are working to create time within the school day.

As important as these strategies are for creating more time for professional development, even these efforts have limits. Thus, it is important to look closely at the ways teachers can learn and improve their practice while they work. Figure 5.1 presents an array of job-embedded learning opportunities teachers identified in their daily work.

Many of these informal learning structures/activities listed would fall under the category of teaching acts, both supportive and intellectual. Most, however, belong to the enterprise of teaching—all of those things teachers normally do while teaching. There are two dimensions in the matrix displayed. The horizontal axis represents the degree of structure in the learning opportunity. For example, talking with colleagues is generally informal and unstructured while conducting collaborative action research is systematic and requires more structure and coordination. The vertical axis represents individual versus collaborative learning. Reading articles and books is categorized as an individual learning activity. Serving on a committee is a collaborative work activity.

Together the two dimensions create four general types of learning opportunities in teachers' work. *Individual Informal* (upper left) contains activities that are generally informal and individual occasions for learning. *Individual Structured* (upper right) lists more structured/coordinated learning activities for individuals. In *Collaborative Informal* (lower left) the activities tend to be informal and collaborative. *Collaborative Structured* (lower right) contains collaborative activities that generally require more structure and coordination.

Before I provide a brief description of each quadrant, there are several caveats about Figure 5.1 for the reader to consider. The list of activities is not novel or surprising to anyone in education; they are simply ordinary occasions in teachers' daily routines that offer great potential for professional growth. The examples listed are not exhaustive of all the possibilities for teacher learning on the job. The placement of teaching activities into various quadrants is a generalization and a convenience for purposes of illustration, not an absolute. The figure is meant to be suggestive and descriptive. Thus, reading articles and books is an individual informal activity in the figure but could be easily be classified as a collaborative activity in schools where professional reading circles have been established. Or, mentoring may be a structured induction program in one school and be very informal in another. Regardless of where any individual activity has been placed in the figure, the important message is that the work of teachers in schools provides many occasions for professional learning and growth.

Individual Informal

> There are many opportunities if you choose to take it, depending on your time management. I personally do a lot of reading, and again in newspapers and magazines I find current issues that make lessons more valid to kids. I go into classrooms and observe the kids in other classes (junior high school teacher, 25 years of experience).[10]

The self-contained classroom continues to dominate public schools. As a result, teachers have learned to rely on a variety of *individual informal* learning opportunities in their work to gain new knowledge, strengthen skills, and improve their professional practice. Perhaps the most powerful of these learning opportunities is reflection "in" and "on" teaching. A number of scholars provide extensive detail and analysis of the contributions of reflection to growth, learning, and enhancement of professional practice.[11]

Individual informal learning activities also include reading, surfing the Internet, and viewing videos. Time for these activities varies greatly across classrooms, schools, and levels. There often are dramatic differences in "free/preparation time" between elementary teachers and high school teachers. Classroom teaching also provides multiple opportunities to experiment with instructional strategies, try out new ideas, examine student work, create student learning activities, observe students, and make hundreds of decisions affecting instruction, learning, discipline, and classroom management and see the consequences of those choices.

Individual Structured

In some cases, teachers engage in work activities that have a built-in structure requiring more systematic organization and coordination of people, materials, and resources. For example, teachers who conduct classroom action research engage in the systematic collection and analysis of data to address a particular concern. All teachers collect and analyze data. The difference here is a structure that organizes the process in ways that support both action and continuous professional learning while teachers carry out their normal teaching duties. Other examples of individual structured work activities that support teacher learning include participation in self-studies (generally guided by specified protocols), analyzing student test data, creating and maintaining portfolios, writing action plans, developing individual professional development plans, writing grants, and writing for publication.

Collaborative Informal

For one elementary teacher with 14 years of experience, interacting with her colleagues is the primary way she continues to get better at her teaching:

The biggest thing again to me is to work it out with someone else, whether it be the co-worker or whether it's my principal or you know someone from administration who's a program support teacher or whatever the area is. You know, I think you can self-evaluate and you can critique what you've done on your own and I think that's valuable and certainly there's a time when that's the most appropriate. But for me, I think it's most helpful to again bounce ideas off each other and evaluate at least a team, I mean in a partnership if not a small team, and I have a pretty good principal for that. And again, I have a really nice cohesive group that everyone is very good about. It's great! It makes a huge difference and nobody feels criticized if you say, "Hey, you know what I would have tried on that?" It's just, like, perfect and we learn from each other whether it's, oh my gosh, you know, we'll plan it together and then we'll go and implement it and even though we planned it together the implementation can look completely different and we come back and evaluate. "That's great, next time I'm going to try that." So I think it's just really key to share your ideas with other people and you share your strategies.[12]

In professional learning communities, teachers rely on *collaborative informal* learning to induct and socialize new staff, gain craft knowledge, improve instruction, build collective capacity, and deal with sundry workplace issues. Talk is the primary vehicle for this learning. But as the teacher above notes, this is more than idle chatter. The talk is increasingly concrete, specific, and focused on collegial sharing and evaluating to improve practice that supports student learning. Interactions with colleagues on joint projects, in meetings, sharing information from professional conferences, observing and critiquing other teachers, and talking to students about their learning are all ways teachers work together to enhance their professional expertise.

Collaborative Structured

In addition to actual instruction in classrooms, teachers work with colleagues in a variety of collaboratively structured activities to realize individual and collective educational goals. Each has the potential to support both individual and collective learning in schools. Team/collaborative teaching is a highly effective instructional strategy as well as a powerful professional learning experience. Let us use the elementary teacher's comments cited in the collaborative informal learning section above. Imagine for a moment what she might have said if she were team teaching, a collaborative structured learning opportunity. To illustrate, I will paraphrase her remarks to highlight likely differences between structured and informal professional development opportunities.

Team teaching also combines a number of different collaborative structured learning opportunities. For instance, working together teachers collaboratively design curriculum, assess student learning, and develop new instructional plans. Team teaching also fosters professional interdependence and mutual support. Peer observation, colleague consultation and feedback, mentoring, and coaching are other collaborative structured learning opportunities for teachers working in teams.[13]

LIMITATIONS TO JOB-EMBEDDED LEARNING

Notwithstanding the advantages to professional development "in" work, there are some potential problems with job-embedded learning. Cognitive

For us, it's helpful to again bounce ideas off each other and evaluate them as a team. It's a partnership. We have a pretty good principal for that. And again, we have really nice cohesive teams and everyone is very good about it. It's great! It makes a huge difference and nobody feels criticized if your teaming partner or other teams say, "Hey, you know, what we would have tried on that?" It's just like perfect and we learn from each other. Whether it's, oh my gosh! You know we'll plan it together and then we'll go and implement it. Even though we planned it together in grade-level teams, the implementation may look completely different across various partner teams. In weekly meetings we come back, evaluate, and talk about successes and problems. People say, "What you guys did sounds great, next time we could try that." So what's really key to our professional learning during the school day is to share ideas and strategies with other people.

psychologists tell us that prior knowledge and experience may actually hinder new learning. Prior knowledge is often a scaffold to new insights and understandings. However, it can also be a psychic prison. As Dewey reminded us decades ago, not all experiences are educative ones.[14] They are mis-educative if their ultimate effects arrest or distort growth and learning. Thus, current practices and understandings of professional work may filter out or distort possibilities for new learning and improved practice.

A second potential limitation to job-embedded learning is that not all educators have the disposition and capacity to learn from and in their work. Professional learning in work requires the capacity to reflect, analyze, interpret, and integrate prior knowledge, current realities, and new information into an emerging and dynamic body of professional expertise and knowledge while simultaneously carrying out normal work routines. This is no easy task. Thus, an over-reliance on job-embedded learning could be frustrating, and even futile, for practitioners who lack reflective skills.

Designers of learning environments work to bring together optimal conditions for learning. Unfortunately, some school and community environments are negative cultures characterized by cynicism, open hostility to new ideas and demands, lack of collective commitment, and high levels of emotional toxicity that contaminate the work/learning environment. Such conditions stifle informal, job-embedded learning for teachers and principals. Surviving the workday becomes more important than professional enrichment and improved practice.

Unless the school and staff are guided by a powerful sense of professional commitment and organizational purpose, professional development "in" work, which is often informal and unstructured learning, tends to be less responsive to specific learning needs, goals, and school priorities. Last, without a shared sense of organizational purpose to guide professional energies, there is always the possibility that professional development "in" work may reinforce teacher isolation as well as fragmentation and incoherence in professional learning. So then, what are some of the motivators and barriers to creating environments that support professional development "in" work?

MOTIVATORS AND BARRIERS TO PROFESSIONAL DEVELOPMENT "IN" WORK

One way to think about the factors included in Table 5.1 is a force-field analysis. That is, motivators are factors that create positive forces that support teacher learning "in" work. Barriers are forces that hinder on-the-job learning. Force-field analysis suggests two possible strategies for building supportive environments for professional development "in" work. The first strategy is to increase the force and intensity of motivating factors. For instance, the social support and collegial interactions among teachers that come from opportunities to learn "in" work provide an important set of incentives to maintain conditions that support collaborative learning "in" work. By highlighting these factors, and making them a part of cultural expectations and norms, learning in work will thrive and expand. System rewards and structures combined with these intrinsic factors also are systematic ways to create and maintain optimal conditions for learning and growth in professional work.

There are numerous examples of successful strategies schools/districts have developed to enhance motivators that support professional development "in" work. Let us examine several of the motivators cited in Table 5.1 and the ways these motivators are used to support professional learning.

Social Interaction. Increasing opportunities for social interaction among teachers and administrators creates multiple opportunities for them to learn from one another by talking about their experiences, reflecting on practice, and sharing acquired professional wisdom. Providing the physical spaces away from classrooms, adequate time, and easy access to technology (e.g., telephones, computer, and fax machines) for these interactions enhances social interaction, decreases isolation, and makes the school a more humane environment. Enhancing social interaction requires resources: sometimes these are new; other times they are reallocated resources.

Colleague Support. Mentoring and peer support programs for new teachers and administrators support learning in schools by tapping into the wealth of experience and expertise colleagues can share with one another.[15]

Situated Cognition/Transfer. Colleague demonstrations of new practice, presentation of information within school in settings where new knowledge

Table 5.1   Professional Learning "In" Work: Motivators and Barriers

Motivators
- Social interaction
- Intrinsic value, personal enrichment
- Sense of professional responsibility
- Colleague support
- Positive culture–professional learning community
- Relevant to work and professional needs
- Situated cognition & ease of transfer
- Rewards & structures that support it
- Positive disposition toward learning & school improvement
- High personal and professional efficacy

Barriers
- Lack of time and energy
- Role overload and work-related stress
- Lack of information
- Lack of personal interest and skills
- It is hard work
- Personal issues—life, family
- Negative school culture
- Low personal and professional efficacy

will be put into practice, tuning protocol processes, and critical friend groups are excellent venues for situating the learning close to where it will be put into practice.

Intrinsic Value and Personal Enrichment. Helping teachers and administrators renew their commitment to their professional work and reconnect to those factors that animate and give meaning to their daily routines is also an important motivator for professional growth and development. Reflective journal writing, special interest work groups, and collaborative inquiry are supportive activities. Affirmation of the work (paying attention to the work of others), rituals and ceremonies to celebrate success, and formal and informal opportunities to share joys and concerns are ways to affirm educators as people and to recognize the intrinsic worth of their professional commitment and daily work.

In force-field analysis, an alternative strategy is to reduce the occurrence and impact of barriers that hinder learning in work. This may include such strategies as the creative use and allocation of time, the reduction of innovation and role overload (too many changes with too many competing priorities), and working to mitigate numerous negative aspects of culture that feed cynicism and sap professional energy and esprit. What do removal of barrier strategies look like in practice?

Lack of Time. Adjusting calendars, clocks, and schedules helps to remove "lack of time" as a barrier to professional learning "in" work. Creating time by using substitutes to free up individuals or groups of teachers, extending contacts into the summer months, using daily scheduling of classes to create common planning and collaborative work time, as well as restructuring the school day through early release, late starts, or banking are major time creation strategies.

Lack of Interest and Skills. Pre-assessment of the learning conditions may indicate that individuals lack interest or requisite knowledge and skills to take advantage of learning opportunities. On the issue of disinterest, it is important to identify the source of disinterest. It could come from a lack of information and awareness. In this case, it would be important to provide multiple venues and opportunities to acquire more information and identify key people for consultation. It is also possible that lack of interest stems from perceived, or perhaps real, lack of input and control into the direction and content of learning. The use of individual professional improvement plans linking individual interests to organizational goals directly addresses this issue and puts the responsibility for professional learning in the hands of the professional.

Why is it that some teachers can find numerous occasions for professional learning and improvement through workplace experiences while others struggle to survive the demands of their daily work? There are no simple answers to that question. Individual capacity and understanding of the role of a professional are two key factors. Teachers who take charge of their learning and see it as a professional responsibility are predisposed to spontaneously converting work experiences and events into occasions for learning. This is not easy given the intensity of the teacher's workday and it requires the development of a number of skills. Teachers and principals need awareness of their actions and the consequences of those actions. They also must develop skills to reflect, analyze, and interpret as they carry out their professional routines. Teachers and principals in professional learning communities must also work together to develop their capacity for collective reflection. It is through collective reflection that educators commit to shared goals, create shared meaning, and develop collective professional capacity that positively influences student learning.

CONCLUSION

At the outset of this book, I proposed a definition of professional development that included three major criteria. *Professional development refers to learning opportunities that engage teachers' creative and reflective capacities in ways that strengthen their practice.* To what degree does professional development "in" work meet these criteria? First, as indicated in Figure 5.1, the array of daily activities embedded in the *enterprise* and *acts* of teaching provide countless occasions for professional learning—whether they are informal or structured, individual or collective. Second, depending on individual and collective capacity, each of these ordinary, and sometimes routine, activities has the potential to engage teachers' creative and reflective capacities. Finally, there is ample evidence that the primary reason teachers commit themselves to continuous learning, and develop the skills for reflective practice, is to enhance student learning and development by enhancing their own expertise and practice.

As you consider the new architecture for professional development, think about opportunities for professional learning "in" work at your school. Is professional development "in" work a significant and recognized part of the professional learning culture? What evidence is there to support your assessment? How might occasions for professional learning "in" work be enhanced? There are other major venues for teacher learning. Next, we will examine professional development "at" work.

SITE VISITS

www.edweek.org
Education Week
www.pacificnet.net/~mandel
A homepage by teachers, for teachers. It is a free, nonprofit service. It costs nothing to access the information, and no money is made from teachers who contribute. Material on this service is updated weekly during the school year.
www.middleweb.com
Exploring Middle School Reform is produced by the Focused Reporting project with grant support from the Program for Student Achievement of the Edna McConnell Clark Foundation.
www.ed.gov/NLE
National Library of Education (NLE) is the world's largest federally funded library devoted solely to education. NLE is the federal government's main resource center for education information.
www.ed.gov/free
FREE is the collective effort of more than thirty federal agencies working together to make hundreds of federally supported teaching and learning resources easier to find.

SUPPLEMENTARY READING

Glatthorn, A. A., & Fox, L. E. (1996). *Quality teaching through professional development.* Thousand Oaks, CA: Corwin Press.
Joyce, B., & Showers, B. (1995). *Student achievement through staff development* (2nd ed.). White Plains, NY: Longman.

Loucks-Horsley, S., Hewson, P. W., Love, N., & Stile K. E. (1998). *Designing professional development for teachers of science and mathematics.* Thousand Oaks, CA: Corwin Press.

Novick, R. (1996). Actual schools, possible practices: New directions in professional development. *Educational Policy Archives Analysis, 4*(14), 1-18.

Osterman, K. F., & Kottkamp, R. B. (1993). *Reflective practice for educators: Improving schooling through professional development.* Thousand Oaks, CA: Corwin Press.

Schon, D. A. (1983). *The reflective practitioner: How professionals think in action.* New York: Basic Books.

Schon, D. A. (1987). *Educating the reflective practitioner.* San Francisco: Jossey-Bass.

NOTES

1. Novick, R. (1996). Actual schools, possible practices: New directions in professional development. *Education Policy Archives Analysis, 4*(14), 1–18.

2. Used with permission. Excerpt from interview transcript for 2001 class project. EDAD 847. University of Wisconsin-Madison.

3. This categorization of teaching comes from the work of Paul Komisar (1968). Teaching: Acts and enterprise. In C. J. B. MacMillan & T. W. Nelson. (Eds.), *Concepts of teaching: Philosophical essays.* Chicago: Rand McNally. As cited in an excellent article by Brent Kilbourn. (1991). Self-monitoring in teaching. *American Educational Research Journal, 28*(4), 721–736.

4. Rubenson, K., & Schutze, H. G. (1995). Learning at and through the workplace: A Review of participation and adult learning theory. In D. Hirsch, & D. A. Wagner (Eds.), *What makes workers learn: The role of incentives in workplace education and training.* Cresskill, NJ: Hampton Press.

5. Stern, D. (1998). Situated learning in adult education. *ERIC Digest 195*, 3. Columbus, OH: ERIC Clearinghouse on Adult Career and Vocational Education.

6. Knowles, M. (1984). *The adult learner: A neglected species* (3rd ed.). Houston, TX: Gulf.

7. Schon, D. A. (1987). *Educating the reflective practitioner.* San Francisco: Jossey-Bass.

8. Used with permission. Except from interview transcript for 2001 class project. EDAD 847. University of Wisconsin-Madison.

9. National Foundation for the Improvement of Education. (1996). *Teachers take charge of their learning.* Washington, DC: Author.

10. Used with permission. Except from interview transcript for 2001 class project. EDAD 847. University of Wisconsin-Madison.

11. Schon, D. A. (1983). *The reflective practitioner: How professionals think in action.* San Francisco: Jossey-Bass; Osterman, K. P., & Kottkamp, R. B. (1993). *Reflective practice for educators: Improving schools through professional development.* Newbury Park, CA: Corwin Press.

12. Used with permission. Except from interview transcript for 2001 class project. EDAD 847. University of Wisconsin-Madison.

13. Bambino, D. (2002). Critical friends. *Educational Leadership, 59*(6), 25–27.

14. Dewey, J. (1938). *Experience and education.* New York: Macmillan.

15. See, for example, mentoring programs for new teachers and principals: Grow Our Own Principals, First-Year Principals, other mentoring examples around the nation. Retrieved July 1, 2002 from www/madison.k12.wi.us/hr/GOOP.htm

6

Professional Development "At" Work

Learning at work has become one of the most exciting areas of development in the dual fields of management and education.[1]

INTRODUCTION

In Chapter 5, we looked at opportunities for professional development "in" work. These included four major types of job-embedded learning: individual informal, individual formal, collaborative informal, and collaborative formal professional learning activities. Within the demands of their daily work in schools, teachers and principals have a variety of occasions to enhance individual skills and improve their professional practice. In this chapter, I describe a related, yet distinct, area of professional development for teachers—professional development "at" work.

To state the obvious, when teachers teach they develop a rich background of direct experiences that, when reflected upon and analyzed, contribute to improved practice and ongoing growth. There are countless opportunities to enhance professional knowledge, skills, and practice. Thus, in one respect the activities described in Chapter 5 were "at" work learning experiences. However, I wish to make a distinction at this point. For teachers, professional development "in" work referred to learning opportunities embedded in the work activities themselves—both the enterprise tasks of teaching and the supportive and intellectual acts of teaching. Professional development "at" work, often described in the adult and vocational literature as "workplace learning," describes on-site learning opportunities within the teacher's ordinary workday. "At" work professional development describes learning opportunities that occur at times when teachers are not working directly with students or preparing to teach.

This chapter begins with a brief summary of research findings on workplace learning. In the second section, I describe a variety of "at" work professional learning opportunities. I then turn to ways to create optimal conditions for professional learning "at" work. In the next section I describe the advantages and potential limitations to professional development "at" work. The chapter concludes with a brief discussion of Etienne Wenger's social learning framework and its implications for the creation of professional learning communities in schools.

SURVEYING THE LANDSCAPE OF WORKPLACE LEARNING

There is a significant body of research on workplace learning. Nevertheless, the landscape is not particularly well mapped. This can be explained in part by traditions of research and conceptions of organizational purpose that separated learning from work. Learning has generally occurred in educational institutions and was understood to be preparation *for* work, not an *integral part of work*. More recently, workplace learning has been viewed from a multidisciplinary perspective blurring such traditional boundaries as academic disciplines, organizational types, and methods of inquiry. David Boud and John Garrick provide an excellent example of this cross-disciplinary perspective in *Understanding Learning at Work.* They conclude, "Distinctions between life and work, learning and productions, community and enterprise are becoming less firm. Shifting boundaries, changing values and purposes of work and learning affect the physical, emotional and cognitive demands on workers at all levels."[2] To provide a background for understanding professional development at work, I have selected key ideas and research findings from the work of Boud and Garrick. As you review this synthesis presented in Table 6.1, consider how each is expressed in schools as workplaces and what influence it has for teachers' and principals' learning.[3]

Workplace Learning in Schools

What implications do these findings have for professional development "at" work for teachers? For principals? Let us examine several of the major points. We know, for example, that the work of teachers and principals is complex and requires extensive training, skill development, and

Table 6.1   A Synthesis of Research on Workplace Learning

- Workplace learning is the lifeblood of modern organizations.
- Effective leaders understand the connections between learning and work and act in ways to strengthen these linkages.
- The literature on workplace learning suggests three broad purposes: to improve individual and group work performance for organizational success; to benefit individuals by enhancing their knowledge, skills, and capacity to continue learning; and to improve society by helping individuals gain valuable knowledge, skills, and values that support active citizenship, commitment to community, and engagement in the society's future.
- The context of work—including power relationships, equity, culture, and language—influences how people construct knowledge and what they learn.
- Economics and market forces drive much of the current demand for workplace learning. In addition, there is renewed interest in lifelong learning to promote the development of the "whole person," not just the worker.
- In modern organizations, knowledge is *the* primary resource. Thus, there is an unprecedented demand for learning. Successful organizations create optimal conditions for maintaining this renewable resource.
- Workplace learning contributes to individual and team growth and development.
- The traditional, separate cultures of learning (educational institutions) and work (employment) are substantially different in their views of the world, the languages they use, and their purposes. These differences limit communication and collaboration.
- Because of its location, workplace learning helps transform the purpose, nature, and outcomes of work.
- There is no universal model or design for workplace learning. It is multifaceted and diverse in purpose, design, and delivery.
- Learning is a core part of work, not just a precursor to it.
- Learning at work promotes collaborative processes.
- Not all workplace learning is good. To avoid unintended or negative learning outcomes, it is important to provide guidance, both formal and informal, to support the learner.

refinement. Not all of this can be contained in preprofessional training programs. Consequently, teachers and principals come to their schools with licenses to practice but still needing time and opportunity to continue their learning to develop higher levels of professional expertise. In some states, for example, teachers and principals receive an initial, nonrenewable license upon successful completion of their training programs. In such cases, new licenses are required to continue their professional development, much of it the workplace, before they can receive a professional license.

Policy makers and community members also recognize the importance of professional development to the quality and future of their schools. School improvement plans, innovations, and restructuring initiatives all have significant resources dedicated to professional development. Teachers who are active learners create conditions that nurture student learning and development. School principals, instructional leaders and learners themselves, also play an important role in professional learning at work. They work to create authentic, caring learning environments for everyone in the school. They lend their expertise and support to the design, delivery, and development of content of workplace learning. Last, they systematically evaluate learning outcomes and assess their impact on school priorities and goals.[4] Professional development "at" work is the lifeblood of successful schools.

A Cautionary Note on Workplace Learning in Schools

Not all workplace learning is good. In some cases, for instance, negative cultures in schools adversely affect professional growth and development. Too often, new and inexperienced teachers are given no more than a grade book and the keys to their rooms when they begin their professional careers. To survive, they become quick learners. However, a novice teacher in an impoverished professional learning environment may come away with some harmful lessons. For example, they may learn such ideas as: "Not all students can learn. There is little I can do to overcome the disadvantages of the children's home and community environments. And/or, I can survive this innovation, too; veteran teachers have done it before." To avoid these unintended learning outcomes, schools and the professionals in them identify and articulate core values, set goals, design learning opportunities to meet those goals, and provide the resources to support the learner. Induction programs, peer coaching, mentoring, and teaming are among the strategies used to achieve positive learning outcomes at school.

Professional Development "At" Work: A Familiar Paradigm

Professional development "at" work (Table 6.2) includes activities that most educators associate with traditional staff development and inservice in schools. Because most of a teacher's workday is spent working directly with students or colleagues in preparation and planning for teaching, when does professional development at work take place? Notwithstanding already full workdays, many opportunities for teacher learning and development are squeezed into other parts of the day—before and after school, during release time, and in place of teacher prep-times. Scheduled inservice days, and extra contract days during the summer

Site Visit

www.ncrel.org

Table 6.2   Professional Development "at" Work

Learning Activity	Examples of Professional Development "At" Work in Practice
Workshops	Outside speakers, consultants, special topics, simulations, in-house expert demonstrations and presentations, teacher resource centers.
Training	Just-in-time, skill-building sessions, external consultants, advisors, and facilitators, demonstrations, simulations, practice and coaching sessions, audio/video/digital training materials.
Meetings	Staff, teams, and units, ad hoc, discussion and inquiry groups, video conferencing, colleague consultation, classroom observation and evaluation session with supervisors
On-site classes	Special topics, introduction of new technologies, content, instructional and organizational methods.
Teacher networks	Online networks, content and special project networks, school/university partnerships.
Distance learning	Self-guided, informal learning, e.g. surfing the Internet, formal classes.
Electronic connections	Electronic portfolios, e-mail, online bulletins boards, networks, exchanges.
In-school exchanges	Peer observations, classroom visits, informal collaboration, team sharing.

months, provide other times for professional development "at" work. These activities individually, or in combination with others, provide multiple opportunities for learning at work.

While these activities may be familiar ones to teachers and principals, many educators have mixed feelings regarding their value based on negative personal experiences. This suggests an intriguing paradox. The professional development activities listed above have both great promise and potential problems. Various educational reform papers and policy documents, to name a few sources, claim that professional development—including many of the activities listed above—is the key to raising student achievement, implementing high academic standards, implementing organizational change, transforming failing schools, improving instruction, and creating authentic professional learning communities. On the opposing view, however, is a stinging critique of traditional staff development and teacher inservice activities. Teacher staff development and inservice, "as generally practiced, has a terrible reputation among scholars, policy makers, and educators alike as being pedagogically unsound, economically inefficient, and of little value to teachers."[5] In addition, traditional staff development activities are often piecemeal, fragmented, and incoherent;[6] have little impact on teachers' instructional practices;[7] not embedded in teachers' daily work routines;[8] focus on narrow, decontextualized technical skills and often lacking connections to deeper content and pedagogical knowledge and professional beliefs;[9] poorly evaluated;[10] and generally fail to provide adequate follow-up resources and support to sustain changes in teacher practices and school structures.[11]

So then, when we consider these activities included in professional development "at" work, how do we deal with this paradox? The uncertainties that paradoxes introduce may also contain ideas for ways of dealing with persistent contradictions and dilemmas in professional development and practice. Recognizing and living with the fact that professional development has the potential to be simultaneously promising and problem-laden forces us to move out of the traditional box that may limit our thinking. Dealing with the paradoxes of professional development requires us to ask new questions, turn ideas and practice upside down, reframe issues, and look for surprises.

CREATING OPTIMAL CONDITIONS FOR WORKPLACE LEARNING

There are numerous opportunities for professional development at work. In healthy learning environments, teachers and administrators find creative ways to encourage and support professional development during the workday. However, not all educators find themselves in environments that encourage and support continuous learning and growth. When favorable conditions for the workplace do not exist, what can be done to move them in the direction of becoming more positive professional learning environments? There is not one model of a learning-enriched school. Nonetheless, authentic, learning-enriched school communities do share a number of common workplace elements that mitigate the negative aspects of professional development described in the previous section. Figure 6.1 organizes these elements into four major areas: (a) the social organization of school; (b) resources; (c) school structures; and (d) individual characteristics. Let us examine each in greater detail.

Social Organization of School

Over the past four decades, research on school culture and professional community suggests that learning-enriched schools share five key elements in social organization that support professional development at work.[12] First, professional learning communities have clearly articulated, shared goals that give coherence and meaning to school improvement, individual professional practice, and learning throughout the organization. Second,

Figure 6.1 Common Workplace Elements in Learning-Enriched Schools

Social organization

School structures   Resources

Individual characteristics

there are multiple expressions of collaboration in professional work and learning through dialogue, joint work, and collaborative planning. Third, teachers and principals develop shared instructional goals and determine strategies for achieving those ends. These goals, especially ones centered on student learning, are powerful organizers that give direction and meaning to individual and collective work while creating the results each professional truly desires. Fourth, shared purpose, collective expertise, and professional interdependence create identity and meaning for everyone in communities of practice. Fifth, trust is a uniting thread across all of these elements of social organization in learning-enriched schools. Learning at work often asks teachers and principals to take risks. Professional learning may involve experimenting with new ideas and practices, changing familiar routines, or suspending judgments about likely outcomes. Steep learning curves may create cognitive dissonance and stress leaving otherwise confident professionals feeling anxious and vulnerable. Like a safety net, an environment of trust provides the psychological, emotional, and interpersonal assurance learners need as they experience both the joys and uncertainties of learning at work.

Resources

Recently, I asked teachers, principals, and other administrators to identify the major factors that limit their professional development in schools. It was no surprise when they said, time and money. Opportunities to learn "at" work are generally less costly than other "off-site" professional development activities. Though there are obvious efficiencies in workplace learning, key resources are required including time, money, materials, facilities, and support personnel. For teachers and principals to develop their professional knowledge and expertise at work, they need time to study, to reflect on what they have learned, and to consult with others.

Some of the most valuable resources available to educators in schools are their professional colleagues. To take advantage of the expertise and experiences of their colleagues teachers need time to meet, talk, and reflect on their learning and practice.[13]

Money is another key resource. Providing an environment that fosters continuous learning and experimentation at work has a number of direct costs. For instance, schools need to purchase materials (books, software, training kits, and videos), pay for consultants, and provide substitute teachers to free up teachers for learning opportunities during the day. Money also provides for the third key resource, an infrastructure of facilities (resource rooms and labs) and equipment (computers and network capability) to support learning at work. Finally, workplace learning requires support personnel who are able, available, and willing to provide guidance, assistance, and support professional development at work.

School Structures. Professional learning communities also share common structural features. Without these supportive structures and processes, opportunities for professional development "at" work would be severely limited. These include the creative use of time, community support, strong leadership, systematic evaluation processes, decentralized decision making for professional development, and the capacity to use structures and make rules work to support professional learning rather than seeing them as major obstacles. Professional learning communities do not permit bureaucratic structures and rigid policies to limit professional growth and organizational improvement. They find ways to work within school board policy, work routines, and negotiated union contracts creating flexibility and opportunity through waivers and side agreements when necessary.

In the previous section, time was described as a critical resource that supports professional learning. Time is also a major structural feature in schools—days, calendars, schedules, and instructional time. Figure 6.2 illustrates five examples of how educators across the country can reorganize or create time for professional development by changing the structure of time during the school day.[14] These five methods are described below:

Freed-up time: Providing substitutes, teaming arrangements, and organizing special events.

Restructured time: Changing the school day (late start, early release, banking time), school calendar, and teaching schedules.

Common time: Organizing teachers' schedules for time to meet, talk, and learn together.

Better-used time: Making better use of currently scheduled meeting times and professional activities.

Purchased time: Hiring additional staff (permanent substitutes and support staff) to free teachers up from teaching or other professional duties.

Figure 6.2   Creating Time for Professional Development

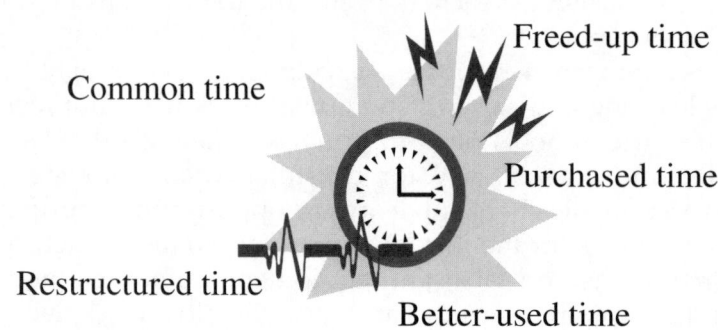

Strong leadership from principals, other administrators, and the school board is also characteristic of schools with powerful norms of professional learning at work. First, professional learning is valued in the organization and is seen as an important dimension of professional work. Second, strong leaders understand it as and at work. Third, leaders are in unique organizational positions to influence the allocation of resources and decisions needed to create conditions that promote workplace learning. Also, leaders often have greater influence on others by what they do, rather than what they say. Leaders who are active learners at work create an environment that nurtures, recognizes, and supports professional learning in the workplace.

When educators reorganize their work and school structures to support professional learning at work, it is important that they have the support of parents and the community. Changes in school schedules and calendars that result in children going to school later in the day or coming home earlier can create hardships for parents, many of whom have work schedules that may not be flexible. Thus, many schools in partnership with other community agencies have designed alternative programs for children that meet the needs for staff development time at school and provide quality care for children if needed. Partnerships among educators, parents, and community agencies provide opportunities to work together to create structures and support for on-site learning during regular school days.

Finally, decision making and evaluation are important structures that support professional learning. In schools with multiple opportunities for workplace learning, the decision-making structures and processes for professional development are decentralized. Because workplace learning is often informal and highly individualized, decisions about the design, content, and learning activities are best made by those most directly affected—teachers. Formative and summative evaluations of teachers and principals are also occasions to explicitly link the assessment of professional work to professional development, student learning, and school improvement plans.

Individual and Team Characteristics

Individual characteristics also influence the quality and outcomes of professional development at work. Learners must value and be committed to continuous learning in, at, and through their work. Teachers and principals must also have the capacity to think deeply and critically about their professional knowledge and work. Learners bring their prior knowledge and skills to new learning opportunities. Reflection, analysis, application, and interpretation are requisite skills for integrating new knowledge into current practice. Finally, teachers and principals as members of learning communities need the interpersonal capacity to work and learn together. Workplace learning involves individuals and groups coming together intentionally to support each other in the process of learning.

WORKPLACE LEARNING: PROMISES AND PROBLEMS

Professional development "at" work promises a rich array of learning opportunities for teachers and principals. At the same time, there are a number of potential limitations. I begin by describing reasons why professional development "at" work strengthens learning and improved practice in schools. To begin, there are some obvious efficiencies in terms of resources. Direct costs associated with travel, accommodations, and registration fees are avoided. Also, much of the learning is self-regulated and relies on local expertise, thus reducing the cost for external consultants and advisors. Because the learning activities are on-site, teachers and principals save time. Because time is a critical resource, time saved by not traveling means more time for professional learning activities. On-site learning facilitates the transfer and application of new knowledge and skills. Professional development activities located within teachers' immediate work context tend to be relevant, practical, and directly applicable to work demands and career goals. Though some workplace learning is designed for everyone, the range of activities presented in Table 6.2 accommodates different learning styles, unique needs and interests, and varying levels of professional expertise and development. Professional development "at" school also taps into the collective knowledge, expertise, experiences, and wisdom of professionals in the school. As mentioned earlier, many of the ideas and solutions to persistent challenges in teaching and school leadership are not somewhere outside the school waiting to be recognized; they are already in the school in the collective capacity of highly committed and expert professionals. Last, professional development "at" work provides countless opportunities to build collaborative, interdependent relationships among teachers and administrators that strengthen the school's capacity for self-renewal and improvement while reducing isolation.

While there are many advantages to professional learning at work, there are some potential pitfalls as well. It is possible that people will learn things at work that are not positive. Without appropriate guidance for learners, resources and structures to support positive growth, and core values centered on a commitment to student learning, professional development at work could be self-indulgent or insular, thereby reinforcing current biases and poor practices. New ideas and perspectives to address problems of practice are often met with cynical "yeah-buts" and "been there, done that" attitudes. Minimizing the power and often times toxic influence that organizational "negaholics" have on the learning environment individuals and groups need to develop effective facilitation skills—including monitoring of behaviors, strategies for problem solving, and opportunities to give voice and honor to individual concerns.

Teachers, administrators, and staff may also learn poor habits, inappropriate behaviors, or take short cuts in their learning about classroom management, instructional strategies, and assessment methods, to name a few. These pitfalls can be completely avoided, or at least greatly minimized, by giving thoughtful attention to the induction and socialization of new teachers and administrators using mentoring programs and by providing support personnel and coaches to provide expert knowledge, emotional and psychological support, and additional resources when needed during the process of change, new learning, and unlearning. There is also the possibility that some highly individualized professional development activities at work might not be connected to school goals and thus lessen collective capacity and norms of interdependence. Without favorable conditions that support professional learning at work, other negative consequences include weak learning outcomes with little impact on professional practice or student learning; the development of negative school cultures with dispirited staff; the steady rise of complacency and mediocrity anchored in low professional efficacy; and abandonment of the profession by idealistic, yet frustrated, novices and career professionals. Individual professional development plans, aligned with system incentives and sanctions, performance evaluations, and school/district priorities, provide important linkages among professional learning "at" work, student learning, and school improvement goals.

CONCLUSION

Etienne Wenger argues that people develop a sense of meaning and identity through active participation in various communities of practice (individual, institutional, and civic). With learning represented as an active, integrating social process, Wenger weaves together four key components—community, practice, meaning, and identity.[15] Each of these components can be used to describe communities of practice in schools. Gaining new knowledge and skills to improve practice that enhances student achievement is a major driving force behind investments in professional development "at" work. Wenger reminds us there are other equally powerful reasons to invest in communities of practice through professional development. "Communities of practice should not be reduced to purely instrumental purposes. They are about knowing, but also about being together, living meaningfully, developing a satisfying identity, and altogether being human."[16] Professional development "at" work provides multiple opportunities to move beyond the narrow confines of instrumental learning in schools. In professional learning communities, teachers, principals, support staff, and students working and learning together find meaning, identity, and a connection to others.

So far, we have examined professional development for teachers and principals "in" and "at" work. The primary argument has been that the daily routines of work provide significant opportunities for professional learning, growth, and improved practice. Learning "in" and "at" work is a key dimension of what it means to be a professional. In the next two chapters, I describe the landscape of professional learning "outside of" and "beyond" work.

SITE VISITS

www.education-world.com
Education World: Comprehensive site for educators.
www.libraryspot.com
LibrarySpot: This library resource brings the best library and reference sites together.
www.pbs.org
PBS Online: Teacher information about their specials and regular programming.

The following sites are regional educational laboratories and research centers that educators can access to expand their professional learning opportunities.

www.ael.org
Appalachian Educational Laboratory (AEL)
Specialty: rural education.
www.ncrel.org
North Central Regional Educational Laboratory (NCREL)
Specialty: technology.
www.nwrel.org
Northwest Regional Educational Laboratory (NWREL)
Specialty: school change processes.
www.wested.org
Western Regional Educational Laboratory (WestEd)
Specialty: assessment and accountability.
www.mcrel.org
Mid-Continent Regional Educational Laboratory (McREL)
Specialties: curriculum, learning, and instruction.

www.prel.org
Pacific Region Educational Laboratory (PREL)
Specialty: language and cultural diversity.
www.lab.brown.edu
Northeast and Islands Laboratory at Brown University (LAB)
Specialty: language and cultural diversity.
www.temple.edu/lss
Mid-Atlantic Laboratory for Student Success (LSS)
Specialty: urban education.
www.serve.org
SouthEastern Regional Vision for Education (SERVE)
Specialty: early childhood education.
www.sedl.org
Southwest Education Development Laboratory (SEDL)
Specialty: language and cultural diversity.

SUPPLEMENTARY READING

Boud, D., & Garrick, J. (1999). *Understanding learning at work.* London: Routledge.

Collay, M., Dunlap, D., Enloe, W., & Gagnon, G. W. Jr. (1998). *Learning circles: Creating conditions for professional development.* Thousand Oaks, CA: Corwin Press.

Day, C., Calderhead, J., & Denicolo, P. (1993). *Research on teacher thinking: Understanding professional development.* London: Falmer Press.

Hirsch, D., & Wagner, D. A. (1995). *What makes workers learn: The role of incentives in workplace education and training.* Cresskill, NJ: Hampton Press.

Speck, M., & Knipe, C. (2001). *Why can't we get it right? Professional development in our schools.* Thousand Oaks, CA: Corwin Press.

Wenger, E. (1998). *Communities of practice: Learning, meaning, and identity.* Cambridge, UK: Cambridge University Press.

NOTES

1. Boud, D., & Garrick, J. (1999). *Understanding learning at work.* London: Routledge, 1.

2. Ibid., 4.

3. Ibid.

4. Bredeson, P. V., & Johansson, O. (2000). The school principal's role in teacher professional development. *Journal of In-Service Education, 26*(2), 385–401.

5. Smylie, M. A. (1996). From bureaucratic control to building human capital: The importance of teacher learning in education reform, *Educational Researcher, 25*(9), 9–11.

6. Sparks, D., & Hirsch, S. (1997) *A vision for staff development.* Alexandria, VA: Association for Supervision and Curriculum Development.

7. Little, J. W., Gerritz, W. H., Stern, D. J., Guthrie, J. W., & Marsh, D. D. (1987). *Staff development for California.* Joint publication of the Far West Laboratory for Educational Research and Development (San Francisco) and Policy and Analysis for California Education, University of California-Berkeley, School of Education.

8. Bredeson, P. V. (2000). Teacher learning as work and at work: Exploring the content and contexts of teacher professional development. *Journal of In-Service Education. 26*(1), 63–72.

9. Borko, H., & Putman, R. T. (1995). Expanding a teacher's knowledge base: A cognitive psychological perspective on professional development. In T. R. Guskey & M. Huberman (Eds.), *Professional development in education: New paradigms and practices.* New York: Teachers College Press.

10. Guskey, T. R. (1995). Professional development in education: In search of the optimal mix. In T. R. Guskey & M. Huberman (Eds.), *Professional development in education: New paradigms and practices.* New York: Teachers College Press; Guskey, T. R. (2001). *Evaluating professional development.* Thousand Oaks, CA: Corwin Press.

11. McLaughlin, M. W., & Oberman, I. (1996). *Teacher learning: New policies and practices.* New York: Teachers College Press.

12. See, for example: Rosenholtz, S. J. (1989). *Teachers' workplace: The social organization of schools.* New York: Longman. Mitchell, C., & Sackney, L. (2001). *Building capacity for a learning community.* Paper presented at the International Congress for School Effectiveness and Improvement in Toronto, Canada.

13. For a complete description of these strategies and examples of their use in schools see *Time Strategies.* (1994). National Education Association.

14. Ibid.

15. Wenger, E. (1998). *Communities of practice: Learning, meaning, and identity.* Cambridge, UK: Cambridge University Press.

16. Ibid., 134.

7

Professional Development "Outside" of Work

Ironically, sometimes the only way teachers and principals can find the time to work together is to leave their schools.[1]

INTRODUCTION

In previous chapters, the focus was on opportunities for professional development "as," "in," and "at" work. In this chapter, we explore opportunities of professional learning "outside" of work. Because neither teaching nor learning is confined to spaces within walls of classrooms and schools, it is important to consider factors beyond teachers' and principals' routine work that provide a wide variety of occasions for deepening professional knowledge, strengthening skills, and developing greater individual and collective expertise. The chapter begins with a definition of professional development "outside" of work and provides examples of various professional learning activities outside of school. Next, I describe common barriers and limitations to professional development opportunities outside of school and identify strategies schools use to address these limitations. The third section builds on these strategies and describes in greater detail how successful learning communities create and support

Table 7.1   Professional Development "Outside" of Work

- Conventions, conferences, and workshops
- Exchanges, site visits
- Sabbatical leaves, study tours
- Retreats
- Special training sessions
- University courses, distance education
- Virtual professional networks
- Professional association meetings, presentations, attendance, participation in governing bodies
- External review panels, task forces, partnerships with business and industry
- Summer programs, institutes
- Funded research projects, collaborative research with universities
- Participation in union activity—negotiations, training, research, advocacy
- Self-study—books, journals, other media
- Any combination of one or more of these activities

professional development outside of work. The final section of the chapter describes how school learning communities share new knowledge, foster team learning, and build organizational capacity from individual and collective professional development activities outside of work.

WHAT IS PROFESSIONAL DEVELOPMENT "OUTSIDE" OF WORK?

Professional development "outside" of work refers to learning activities that are "off-site" and are not a part of a teacher's or principal's ordinary work routines or responsibilities. There are few surprises contained in the list of activities in Table 7.1. Most are familiar ones to teachers and principals. What may be less well understood, however, is how such opportunities can be incorporated into a larger, more integrated design for professional development in schools. By definition and design, these activities are decentralized, individualized, diffuse in focus, and uncertain in terms of outcomes for individuals and their schools. Professional development "outside" of work includes a wide range of activities. Conventions, workshops, and university courses are structured and formal activities. There are also informal activities with less obvious and intentional objectives. These include self-study, sabbatical leaves, and virtual professional networks.

At first glance, the selected listing of activities in Table 7.1 suggests that professional development outside of work is a mixed blessing. On the one hand, various learning opportunities tap into a wealth of critical experiences, knowledge, and expertise well beyond the traditional boundaries of schools. The variety of topics, venues, and experts provides opportunities to differentiate professional development in ways that meet individual needs and different learning styles. Off-site learning also helps to break down the physical and psychological isolation for teachers and principals by permitting interactions with other adults. Social interaction with professionals in education and outside the field often leads to new professional connections and networks—both informal and formal.

On the other hand, there is the possibility that without clear purpose, goals, and design, these activities will be nothing more than incoherent, fragmented, and limited professional experiences. In the next section, I present persistent and troublesome barriers and limitations to professional development outside of work and suggest strategies to address these barriers. In the section that follows, we will examine in greater detail what professional learning communities do to create and support professional growth and development "outside" of work.

BARRIERS TO PROFESSIONAL DEVELOPMENT "OUTSIDE" OF WORK

Notwithstanding the advantages and countless possibilities for professional development outside of work, it is important to understand that there are problems and barriers that limit the quality and impact of various off-site learning opportunities. In Table 7.2, the column on the left lists the five dimensions of professional development. The center column summarizes common barriers and problems with off-site learning. The right-hand column identifies strategies used in successful school learning communities to eliminate those barriers or mitigate potentially negative effects they might cause. At this point, it is worth mentioning that many of the limitations and barriers cited in this section, though important within the context of this chapter, are also common problems for professional development generally. Thus, the strategies used to address limitations in professional development "outside" of work also have broader implications for addressing persistent challenges and barriers to professional learning in general.

The list of barriers and limitations contains few surprises for educators; the critique of traditional professional policies and practices has been clearly articulated by many scholars and practitioners.[2] One of the first activities successful professional learning communities engage in is the identification of any factors—structural, cultural, or political—that may be limiting professional development and practice in schools. This list helps us focus on specific strategies and actions to eliminate those limiting factors, or at least reduce their negative impact on professional learning. Dealing with factors that impede professional learning in schools requires a systems thinking approach across five dimensions of professional development.

Table 7.2   Common Barriers and Limitations to Professional Development "Outside" of Work

Professional Development Dimensions	Barriers and Limitations	Strategies Used to Address
Design	Individualistic, opportunistic; Not integrated with other innovations; Not linked to school goals	Systems thinking orientation linking professional learning goals, and innovations Integrated professional development plan—district, school, and individual learning
Delivery	Episodic and fragmented No follow-up Costly—time, money, other resources Passive participation—"sit and get" Limited access and opportunity	Explicit criteria for selecting and sponsoring activities Systematic processes for sharing new knowledge Flexible, creative use of time, money, people, and material
Content	Fragmented and incoherent Quick nuggets of knowledge reducible to workshop formats Focus on application on practice with individual/ group insufficient theoretical support	Explicitly linked to needs and goals school/individual Follow-up strategies to deepen learning: reflection, dialogue, experimentation, collaboration, and feedback
Context	Inadequate resources–time, money Lack of structures to support Negative cultures Daily demands of schools	Multiple strategies to create time, generate resources Intentional plan to create structures and culture to support learning community

(Continued)

Table 7.2 Continued

Professional Development Dimensions	Barriers and Limitations	Strategies Used to Address
Outcomes	Poor assessments of contributions to: Individual learning— knowledge/skills School needs Changes in thinking and practice Impact on student learning Lack of feedback professional development Plans and decisions Inadequate cost/benefit analyses	Systematic evaluation of all aspects of professional development Link assessments to plans and goals Assessment is part of professional development design

Next, we examine in detail how professional learning communities create and support professional development outside of work.

CREATING AND SUPPORTING PROFESSIONAL DEVELOPMENT "OUTSIDE" OF WORK

The current literature in the area of professional development provides a number of lists that summarize key features of successful designs and practices in schools. Though the frameworks vary, there is general agreement that important features in major five areas—design, delivery, content, context, and outcomes—distinguish successful professional development.[3] Table 7.3 summarizes what we know about features that characterize successful professional development in schools. The features identified are useful for understanding and describing differences between professional learning communities, where learning opportunities are successfully integrated, and schools where these activities often remain fragmented and incoherent learning experiences.

Based on these characteristics, we might ask, "To what degree do opportunities for professional development outside of work in our school reflect these important features?" One way to address this question is to compare

Table 7.3   Characteristics of Successful Professional Development

Professional Development Design
- Active, broad participation by teachers and staff
- Linked to long-range school and district goals
- Based on careful assessment of needs—individual, school, students
- Coherent plan expressing core values, purpose, and goals

Professional Development Delivery
- Active learning opportunities
- Continuous and sustained
- Supported by research and successful practices
- Wide range of activities
- Fosters both individual and team learning
- Appropriate to adult learner/practicing professional

Professional Development Content
- Relevant to primary work
- Deepens professional knowledge (content and pedagogical) and skills
- Leads to improved practice
- Connected to other aspects of teachers' work lives

Professional Development Context
- Adequate and continuous resources to support learning
- Time, money, materials, support personnel, opportunity, and space
- Supportive structures—policies, processes, and practices
- Opportunities to share new knowledge and experiment with new ideas, practices
- Supportive learning environment—affirming culture reflecting core values, commitments, and goals

Professional Development Outcomes
- Effective assessments focused on key outcomes
- Enhanced knowledge and skills
- Improved practice
- Learning outcomes of students
- Goal achievement
- Cost/benefit analyses
- Other consequences for individual, school, district, and its stakeholders
- Feedback mechanisms

professional learning communities, where professional development outside of work is an important contributor in enhanced professional and improved practice, with schools where these activities often remain fragmented, individualized, and incoherent learning experiences.

Integrative/Connected Designs

In professional learning communities, professional development is the lifeblood of individual and organizational growth and improvement. In these schools, the designs for professional learning, and their connections to organization mission and priorities, are intentional and clearly articulated. One of the most prominent features of these designs is coherence. Individual and organizational professional plans are linked explicitly to core values and commitments that promote and support all student learning, high standards of professional practice, and continuous learning and improvement. Integrative professional development designs transform seemingly diffuse and opportunistic off-site learning activities into professional experiences that support individual growth and organizational improvement. Professional development designs that link the wide-ranging learning activities listed in Table 7.1 to organizational priorities and resources strengthen the impact on individual learners and increase the likelihood of achieving desired school outcomes. Rather than trying to be gatekeepers of professional learning, schools with integrative designs for professional development provide opportunities for it. The important point here is that coherent professional development designs do not limit professional learning opportunities, they provide direction and purpose that strengthen those experiences.

Unfortunately, the experiences of many educators suggest that coherent designs for professional development are not necessarily the norm in schools. Most teachers and principals participate regularly in various off-site professional activities. However, most schools lack a coherent design for professional development. With the exception of policy statements regarding paid and unpaid leaves, reimbursement for expenses, and the availability of substitutes, there is little to guide teachers' professional development choices and participation other than individual goals and priorities. Thus, while individuals may gain new knowledge and skills, the overall impact on organizational capacity and school outcomes is left to chance.

Delivery and Content

Teachers and principals have a significant influence over the delivery of professional development activities outside of work. As consumers, planners, participants, and evaluators, they can influence the quality and modes of professional development delivery. Professional development activities outside of work are as varied in delivery as they are in type. Delivery options include conventions with thousands of participants, staff retreats, institutes, virtual networks, and, individual self-study to name a few. Regardless of the numbers involved, or the settings in which the activities occur, research indicates that the most effective professional development involves active learning; is delivered using a variety of training strategies; is appropriate to the needs and interests of adult professional learners; includes opportunities for individual and team learning; is intensive and sustained over time; and finds support in research and model practices in real schools.

Professional learning communities recognize that the complex issues of teaching and learning are not easily dealt with in one-shot workshops where experts proverbially "blow in, blow out, and then blow off." Professional learning that deepens content knowledge, strengthens pedagogical skills, improves practice, and ultimately, enhances student learning outcomes takes time. There are no quick fixes.

Bruce Joyce and Beverly Showers found that teachers need a set of "learning to learn" skills that supports their efforts in moving new knowledge and skills into routine use.[4] These include: (a) persistence (sticking with new ideas and methods even when performance may be awkward at best and outcomes are uncertain); (b) understanding the difficulties in transferring training into practice; (c) recognizing and dealing with the difficulties students may have when new methods and practices are introduced; (d) having a deep conceptual understanding of new behaviors they want to introduce into practice; (e) making productive use of colleague expertise; and (f) flexibility (openness to new ideas, a willingness to experiment, and a capacity for inquiry and reflection).

Teachers' workdays are busy. As noted in previous chapters, opportunities for professional development "in" and "at" work are important occasions for learning. Nonetheless, they are limited. Thus, opportunities to learn outside of work in special institutes and training sessions, during sabbatical leaves, and on data retreats, for example, provide excellent occasions for intensive and sustained learning. When the learning activities are connected to other aspects of teachers' work lives, the experiences are more likely to be integrated successfully into routine practices back in school.

Professional Development Context: Support for Professional Learning "Outside" of Work

There are three primary dimensions of context that support professional development outside of work—a positive learning climate, adequate resources, and support structures. A positive and affirming school environment provides opportunities for various learning activities. The activities listed in Table 7.1 exist independent of schools and their activities. Thus, the issue within schools is whether or not teachers and principals have access and opportunities for professional learning outside their regular work. Bringing new ideas, understandings, and innovative practices into schools is a hallmark of learning-enriched schools. In these schools, teachers and principals understand that being a professional means reflecting on beliefs and practice, seeking out new information, and continually improving one's expertise and practice. The professional learning culture does more than allow professional learning outside of work, it expects and celebrates it in routine practice. There is a high sense of personal and professional efficacy anchored in a spirit of inquiry and possibility.

In negative school cultures, teachers and administrators with low personal and professional efficacy hang onto unproductive practices and ideas. They often dismiss the need for new knowledge and skills believing there is little they can do to make a real difference in student learning outcomes in the school. Some staff actively resist innovation and improvement while others wait passively on the sidelines of engaged professional practice.

The availability and allocation of adequate resources to support professional learning outside of work are elements of the second dimension of professional development context. Professional learning communities find, or in many cases create, the resources (time, money, and opportunity) to strengthen individual and team learning outside of work. Organizational priorities drive individual decisions and school-based allocations of scarce resources to support outside learning opportunities. With literally thousands of possibilities, the problem is not one of finding professional development opportunities beyond the school, the real issue is finding ones that are good investments for meeting teaching and learning priorities.

Last, with adequate resources and supportive cultures, professional learning communities work to create structures that institutionalize opportunities for professional development outside of work.[5] For example, professional learning communities have school and district policies that encourage and fund professional development outside of school. They organize and use time creatively. Calendars with built-in days for professional development and the assignment of duties are key areas for using time flexibly. Professional learning communities also have teacher evaluation procedures that include dimensions of professional development as a major characteristic of performance. There are systematic processes for professional development planning, implementation, and assessment. Finally, professional learning communities find ways for teachers and administrators to share what they have learned away from work. Colleague presentations, demonstrations, information displays, discussion groups, and on-site training sessions are some of the strategies used to transfer individual learning into team learning that builds organizational capacity.

Professional Development Outcomes

Determining whether or not the resources invested in professional development outside of work have been well spent requires focused and rigorous assessment. This may well be one of the least developed areas of professional development in general, and more particularly, professional development outside of work. Much of what teachers and principals need to know and be able to do to perform their jobs well has been left up to them. They determine what they need, decide how to get it, and then pay the cost. Other than assessing the impact of accumulated credits on teacher pay, schools traditionally have done little to evaluate the impact of teacher learning outside of work. For school-sponsored activities outside of work, expectations of participants when they return to work have typically been low or nonexistent.

In professional learning communities, teacher and administrator learning is valued and systematically shared. Teachers and administrators are in charge of their own learning, both inside and outside of work. This does not mean, however, that it is disconnected from school goals and shared commitment to student learning priorities. The structures, culture, and resources that support professional development outside of work align individual teacher needs and priorities with school goals and student learning. Here are some questions teachers and administrators might ask about professional development outside of work:

- In what way(s), if any, did the experience increase your knowledge or improve your professional skills?
- In what way(s), if any, did the learning activity change your thinking and beliefs about your work?
- In what way(s), if any, did the experience stimulate you to experiment with new ideas, methods, or practices?
- How has the learning experience contributed to your professional growth plan?
- How does what you learned contribute to student learning and school goals?
- What are some ways of sharing with others what you've learned?

By addressing these and other questions, teachers, administrators, and planning teams are actively assessing the links between professional development outside of work and its impact on people, collective purpose, and the school's priorities for student learning.

SHARING PROFESSIONAL KNOWLEDGE: TEAM LEARNING

There is little doubt that there are powerful and varied professional learning opportunities for teachers and principals outside of their work in schools. Up to this point in the chapter, the discussion has centered on how schools can create the conditions and opportunities for teachers and administrators to take full advantage of opportunities for professional learning outside of school. The very nature of these "off-site" learning experiences makes them ones are that generally limited to a few individuals or perhaps a small group of teachers. It is important to understand how schools can capitalize on such privatized professional learning. How do new ideas, skills, and practices become part of the school's collective capacity? Team learning, expressed in a variety of formal and informal activities in schools, is one of the ways successful learning communities address these questions. Let us examine what we mean by team learning, how schools build learning teams, and how team learning transforms individual knowledge into collective expertise.

One of the best resources on team learning is a collection of works by Peter Senge.[6] He describes team learning as a process that aligns and develops an organization's capacity to create the results its members truly desire. The concept of team is a familiar one. Each of us has had a number of experiences on teams. One thing we have learned from those experiences is that just because people work side-by-side, or are put into groups, does not mean they are a "team." Our experiences tell us that the difference between successful and unsuccessful teams, whether in schools or beyond, is their ability to align their energies in a common purpose, learn from and about one another, recognize each other's strengths and limitations, and create ways to complement and support each other so that their combined efforts lead to success.

The ways in which successful school learning communities develop strategies to share knowledge and skills from individual professional development outside of school reflect the key elements of team learning described by Senge. First, the choices individual teachers and administrators make for learning beyond the school, though motivated by individual interest, are also aligned with a larger learning agenda for the school. Alignment of professional learning means that teachers have a shared understanding of purpose and priorities that guide their decisions about what is worth their time and how it would contribute to collective capacity. Thus, individual visits to other schools, participation in training workshops, and conference attendance are not simply options for individual enrichment; these activities are aligned with school goals and school priorities.

Second, a hallmark of a professional learning community is its capacity to deprivatize professional knowledge and practice. Teachers and principals learn from one another in their daily interactions. This includes formal presentations, informal conversations about practice modeling, demonstrations, mentoring, reflective dialogues, sharing materials, team teaching, and collaborative work. Team learning thrives in schools where there is mutual respect among colleagues; strong cultures exist to support shared learning; and multiple opportunities are embedded in teachers' ordinary workdays to talk about their work, introduce new ideas, reflect on their practice, and jointly create meaning and understanding around their collective work.

Third, in professional learning communities teachers and administrators recognize each other's strengths and limitations and develop ways to complement each other so that their combined efforts lead to success in meeting shared goals. When the goals and priorities in a school are viewed as individual responsibilities and tasks, people work extraordinarily hard but their efforts are fragmented and diffuse. The idea behind team learning is that by sharing professional knowledge and skills, the combined energies and expertise among faculty have the potential to be much greater than the sum of individual parts. As we think about professional knowledge and expertise in schools, Bill Russell of the Boston Celtics provides us with some insight about the relationship of an individual to a successful team. "[We] were a team of specialists, and like a team of specialists in any field, our performance depended on individual excellence and how well we worked together. None of us had to strain to understand that we had to complement each others' specialties; it was simply a fact, and we all tried to figure out ways to make our combination more effective."[7] Imagine a school where no one had to strain to understand how his or her individual efforts complemented colleagues' expertise and specializations; where everyone tried to figure out ways to work together to be better places for student learning and professional growth. This is the essence of a professional learning community. Team learning transforms individual learning from professional development outside of work into collective capacity. Next, we look at three examples that illustrate how team learning enables teachers and principals to share knowledge from professional development outside of work.

Team Learning in Action: Three Vignettes

Displays and Demonstrations. San Francisco's Exploratorium Museum sponsors an intensive, month-long physical sciences institute during the summer.[8] The museum, renowned for its many interactive exhibits that demonstrate such phenomena as sound waves, inertia, and conductivity, features a variety of hands-on professional development activities for teachers. During the summer institute, participants spend three hours a day working with biologists, physicists, and expert teachers in science and mathematics. In addition to these lab sessions and tutorials, teachers use the museum workshops to build small versions of various museum exhibits. Teachers take their mini-exhibits back to their schools and share what they have learned with colleagues and students. Displays in showcases, formal presentations, teaching demonstrations using the exhibits, and informal exchanges resulting from the displays are low-cost, high-impact strategies for sharing professional knowledge from off-site learning.

Site Visit

www.exploratorium.edu

Poster Sessions. During the past 20 years, teaching graduate courses in educational leadership, I have experimented with ways for students to share with colleagues what they have learned in their individual research or school improvement projects. One of the most interactive expressions of professional sharing is the "poster session." Students prepare posters, usually trifold, stand-alone displays, that visually communicate the key ideas, findings, and topics they addressed. Like poster sessions at large professional conferences, the visual images and information presented on individual posters are invitations to others to engage in conversations around a specific topic. Unlike "sit and get" presentations where the presenter controls the flow, timing, and sequencing of information, poster sessions are truly interactive: They permit participants to initiate the discussion, guide the learning, and connect in ways that may be quite unanticipated by the poster presenter. This is one of the best examples of the presenter truly being *a guide on the side*, not the *sage on the stage*. Poster sessions provide a highly dynamic format where professional colleagues share new knowledge, personal interests, and newly acquired skills.

Training Sessions. One of the more structured activities designed to share professional knowledge and skills back on-site is the training workshop. Because of the costs and logistics of trying to send large numbers of staff for specialized training, schools commonly pay the expenses of one or more key people to receive specialized training. The training-of-trainer model has several major advantages. Once trained, the local trainer is on-site for initial demonstrations and training as well as for follow-up support and coaching over time. We know from research and the wisdom of practice that any substantial changes in teaching or administrative practice require significant periods of time for learners to practice, experiment with ideas, be coached, receive feedback, and ultimately integrate new thinking and strategies with current routines. Investing in the training of local experts facilitates the dissemination of new information and provides critical resources for sustaining effective implementation.

CONCLUSION

Professional development "outside" of work expands the horizons of professional learning opportunities for teachers and administrators. Successful school learning communities find ways to eliminate, or at least mitigate, the effects of common barriers and factors that limit off-site learning. Using a systems thinking approach, learning-enriched schools align the energies and resources across professional development design, delivery, content, context, and outcomes to enhance learning, improve practice, and achieve goals focused on student learning. Finally, professional learning outside of work may be mediated through individuals, but it gains force through team learning focused on shared purpose and commitments.

SITE VISITS

www.nsdc.org
National Staff Development Council
www.ed.gov
U.S. Department of Education
www.ed.gov/inits/teachers/development.html
Helping teachers through high-quality professional development.
www.naesp.org
National Association of Elementary School Principals
www.nassp.org
National Association of Secondary School Principals
www.aft.org
The mission of the American Federation of Teachers, part of the American Federation of Labor-Congress of Industrial Organizations (AFL-CIO), is to improve the lives of members and their families and to give voice to their legitimate professional, economic, and social aspirations.
www.cgsnet.org
The Council of Graduate Schools is dedicated to the improvement and advancement of graduate education. Its members are colleges and universities engaged in research, scholarship, and the preparation of candidates for advanced degrees.
www.distance.gradschools.com
A resource for distance education graduate schools.
www.hol.edu
Heritage OnLine Continuing Education for K-12 Teachers. More than 90 self-paced courses that can be done from home, started at any time, and with one year to complete.
www.uni.edu/profdev
UNI Online Professional Development. The University of Northern Iowa Professional Development for Educators program is committed to providing a high-quality learning environment characterized by excellence in teaching, a personalized learning environment, and a genuine sense of community.
www.ncrtl.msu.edu/about.htm
National Center for Research on Teacher Learning (NCRTL) reflects its innovative vision and the focus of its research. Founded at Michigan State University's College of Education in 1985 with a grant from the Office of Education Research and Improvement, U.S. Department of Education, the center's emphasis is on teacher learning and the center's desire to provide leadership in defining this new area of research.
http://www-gse.berkeley.edu/outreach/bawp/bawp.html
The Bay Area Writing Project (BAWP) is a collaborative program of the University of California at Berkeley and Bay Area schools, dedicated to improving writing and the teaching of writing at all grade levels and in all disciplines. The Project includes an expanding network of exemplary classroom teachers, kindergarten through university, who conduct professional development programs for teachers and administrators throughout the summer and school year. As the flagship site of the National Writing Project; BAWP's program model and design are replicated at 160 colleges and universities throughout the country and five sites internationally.
http://csmp.ucop.edu/
The California Subject Matter Projects (CSMPs) are a professional development network of nine discipline-specific projects. There are 104 sites statewide. The nine projects are listed below:

California Arts Project

California Foreign Language Project

California History-Social Science Project

California International Studies Project

California Mathematics Project

California Physical Education and Health Project

California Reading and Literature Project

California Science Project

California Writing Project

www.dade.k12.fl.us/pers/prodev/tec.htm

The Dade-Monroe Teacher Education Center (TEC) provides professional development training for instructional personnel to enhance their professional growth and to renew their teaching certificates. TEC also sponsors many specialized programs. Among these are professional conferences and seminars, educational travel, supervision of interns, and Summer Intensive Seminars. All courses are offered without charge to participants although in some cases participants may be asked to purchase the book(s).

www.dade.k12.fl.us/pers/prodev/data.htm

The Dade Academy for the Teaching Arts, called DATA, is a professional enhancement program for teachers who teach mathematics, English, science, social studies, foreign languages, or exceptional student education in a middle or senior high school. DATA provides an eight-week externship experience for selected teachers each grading period. The teachers are released from all teaching duties and responsibilities for the grading period in order to work on research projects and attend workshops and seminars on topics related to current issues in education. The program is housed at Miami Beach Senior High School and operates in conjunction with the school program.

www.memphis-schools.k12.tn.us/admin/tlapages/academymission. html

The Teaching & Learning Academy is to guide the professional growth and development of all Memphis City Schools educators through high-quality professional development experiences in effective teaching and learning, innovative leadership, and school redesign for the purpose of ensuring that all students learn to high standards.

Professional development for all employees in Memphis City Schools is coordinated through the Teaching and Learning Academy, a state-of-the-art facility jointly funded by the school district and the community. The school district purchased the facility, while Partners in Public Education, a non-profit organization in Memphis that supports school reform, helped support the renovation. The Academy opened in April 1996 and is one of only a handful of its type in the nation.

www.nhc.rtp.nc.us:8080/tserve/tserve.htm

TeacherServe from the National Humanities Center is an interactive curriculum enrichment service for teachers.

www.ga.unc.edu/NCTA/NCTA/index.htm

The North Carolina Teacher Academy is a professional development program for teachers established and funded by the North Carolina General Assembly. The mission of the Academy is to support continuous learning to the growth of a career teacher by providing quality professional development in the areas of school leadership, instructional methodology, core content, and use of modern technology in order to enrich instruction and enhance student achievement.

www.oregoned.org/teaching_and_learning/index.htm

Oregon Educational Association (OEA)'s Teaching and Learning section of its Web site. OEA's Center for Teaching and Learning focuses on the professional issues that affect OEA members. Licensure, continuing professional development information, training and networking opportunities, and education reform issues fall into this area. Its goal is to ensure highly qualified educators and support professionals in Oregon's public schools.

www.nfie.org/publications/centers.htm

The NEA Foundation for the Improvement of Education.

SUPPLEMENTARY READING

Darling-Hammond, L., & Sykes, G. (Eds.). (1999). *Teaching as the learning profession: Handbook of policy and practice.* San Francisco: Jossey-Bass.

Eraut, M. (1994). *Developing professional knowledge and competence.* London: Falmer Press.

NOTES

1. Bredeson, P. V., & Scribner, J. P. (2000). A statewide professional development conference: Useful strategy or inefficient use of resources? Retrieved July 1, 2002, from http://epaa.asu.edu/epaa/v8n13.html

2. See, for example, Sparks, D., & Hirsch, S. (1997). *A new vision for staff development.* Alexandria, VA: Association for Supervision and Curriculum Development. Little, J. W. (1997). *Excellence in professional development and professional community.* Working paper. Washington, DC: Office of Educational Research and Improvement. Darling-Hammond, L., & Sykes, C. (1999). *Teaching as the learning profession: Handbook of policy and practice.* San Francisco, CA: Jossey-Bass. Lieberman, A. (1995). Practices that support teacher development: Transforming conceptions of professional learning. *Phi Delta Kappan,* April, 591–596.

3. Bredeson, P. V. (2000). Teacher learning as work and at work: Exploring the content and contexts of teacher professional development. *Journal of In-Service Education, 26*(1), 63–72.

4. Joyce, B., & Showers, B. (1995). *Student achievement through staff development: Fundamentals of school renewal* (2nd ed.). White Plains, NY: Longman.

5. Bredeson, P. V. (2001). Negotiated learning: Union contracts and teacher professional development. *Education Policy Analysis Archives, 9*(26). Retrieved July 1, 2002 from http://epaa.asu.edu/epaa/v9n26.html

6. Senge, P. (1990), *The fifth discipline: The art and practice of the learning organization*. New York: Currency Doubleday. Senge, P., Kleiner, A., Roberts, C., Ross, R., & Smith, B. (1994). *The fifth discipline fieldbook*. New York: Currency Doubleday. Senge, P., Kleiner, A., Roberts, C., Ross, R., Roth, G. and Smith, B. (1999). *The dance of change: The challenges to sustaining momentum in learning organizations*. New York: Currency Doubleday

7. Senge, P. (1990). p. 233.

8. Retrieved July 1, 2002, from www.exploratorium.edu

8

Professional Development "Beyond" Work

The connections made by good teachers are held not in their methods but in their hearts—meaning heart in its ancient sense, as the place where intellect and emotion and spirit will converge in the human self.[1]

INTRODUCTION

To state the obvious, the work of teaching and leadership in schools is more than the application of expert knowledge and technical skills. Based on this understanding, the purpose of this chapter is to describe professional development "beyond" work. Professional development beyond work includes various enriching experiences and learning opportunities that are away from work and school, ones that do not relate directly to practice. Professional development beyond work focuses on learning and growth experiences that feed the heart, mind, soul, and passions of teachers and principals. I grant that many of the learning opportunities described in earlier chapters may touch and ignite aspects of these human dimensions, but the primary purpose of professional development "as," "in," "at," and "outside of" work is not directed toward them.

It seems reasonable to ask, Does professional development beyond work meet the criteria used to define professional development in Chapter 2? The answer is unequivocal, Yes. First, avocational interests such as travel, playing in a band, photography, spiritual journeys, and gardening—to name a few—have the potential to be rich venues for learning. Second, our focus is on activities and experiences beyond work that engage the creative and reflective capacities of teachers and principals making those experiences seamless contributions to educators' whole being, not merely disconnected breaks from the demands of routine practice. Third, professional development beyond work influences the quality of professional work by nurturing the human qualities that animate the life and work of teachers and principals.

My own journey across the ill-mapped terrain of personal and professional intersections in teaching and school leadership has been greatly influenced by the work of Parker Palmer. I have listened to him speak on various occasions and have read and reread two of his books, *To Know as We Are Known* and *The Courage to Teach*.[2] In many ways, these works and their impact on me have given me the courage to step out from behind the shield of traditional academic research and writing to explore, with no small sense of vulnerability, the intersection of professional learning, working, and living in this chapter.

A new architecture of professional development emphasizes the importance of designing learning opportunities that nurture the intellectual, emotional, and spiritual dimensions of teachers and principals. In a new architecture for professional learning and growth, professional development beyond work helps create and celebrate wholeness by bringing together educators' inner and outer worlds of work, life, and personal identity. Traditional professional development models, and their accompanying lists of defining characteristics, generally focus on "best practices" to enhance teachers' knowledge, skills, and practice. The purpose of this chapter is to describe how a new architecture for professional development gives attention to the wholeness of teachers and principals transforming their professional learning and the schools in which they work.

BROADENING AND DEEPENING OUR UNDERSTANDING OF PROFESSIONAL DEVELOPMENT

As a child, each of us probably had the experience of meeting teachers or principals in places we did not expect to see them—in supermarkets, at concerts, or even canoeing on a river. For me it seemed strange to see my fifth grade teacher, Miss Gripp, choosing breakfast cereals at the local

Piggy Wiggly. Somehow, I could not believe she had another life beyond Fairview Elementary. Even though we knew teachers and principals were "real people," somehow their other self, their personal self, often remained well hidden from view. The educators often reinforced this naïve view of teachers and principals. Not surprisingly then, traditional professional development has generally been silent on aspects of educators' life and work beyond its technical dimensions. The passions, emotions, heart, and soul that energize teaching and leadership remain in the shadows.

Parker Palmer describes teaching, and I would add leadership, as a daily exercise in vulnerability because each occurs, "at the dangerous intersection of personal and public life."[3] For some teachers and administrators, the tensions and personal costs are too high. They lose heart and give up on their own learning and growth. They find ways to shield themselves from personal affront, disappointment, and ridicule by disconnecting themselves from students, their subjects, and even from themselves. The terms, *burned-out, coast-out, deadwood, and negaholics* are familiar ones to most of us. They describe people we know in schools who are merely play-acting in their professional roles. The have neither the energy nor commitment to deal authentically with the tensions and vulnerabilities in their daily work. In complex organizations such as schools, these characteristics are further reinforced by professional cultures that are uncomfortable and distrustful of the inner terrains of personal truths and identity. How then can professional development beyond work help teachers and principals navigate the treacherous intersections of their personal and professional lives?

The obvious answer is that teachers and principals express in their work who they are. We know, for example, that good teachers successfully negotiate the intersection of personal and professional with joy and confidence. "The courage to teach is the courage to keep one's heart open in those very moments when the heart is asked to hold more than it is able so that the teacher and students and subject can be woven into the fabric of community that learning, and living require."[4] Professional development "beyond" work is anchored in these successes. It is more than techniques, new knowledge, and advanced training. It explores two terrains—those beyond work and those deep within teachers and principals.

Professional development beyond work brings together the sometimes fragmented, other times warring, dimensions of teaching, learning, and living. "To chart the landscape fully, three important paths must be taken—the intellectual, emotional, and spiritual—none can be ignored. Reduce teaching to intellect, and it becomes a cold abstraction; reduce it to emotions, and it becomes narcissistic; reduce it to the spiritual, and it loses its anchor to the world. Intellect, emotion, and spirit depend on one another for wholeness. They are interwoven in the human self and education at its best."[5] We begin our exploration by examining the dimensions of teaching and leadership that make each more than a set of expert competencies and routine performances.

BEYOND TECHNIQUE

Though there are notable exceptions, much of what happens in the name of traditional staff development focuses on strategies and techniques that promise practical and timely solutions to the demands of everyday practice. To test this assertion, simply look at the program of any major professional conference. How much of the program is dedicated to the latest techniques? To best practices? It is understandable that professionals want to acquire systematic procedures, techniques, and ready answers to problems of practice. Teaching and school leadership are very complex and demanding professional roles that require a repertoire of specialized techniques, routinized skills, and habits of practice that help them deal efficiently and effectively with their work.

However, good teaching and effective leadership require more than technique. One only has to observe the differences between novices and experts in their use of particular techniques to understand that highly effective professional practice involves more than the use of the latest techniques. Parker Palmer refers to a common saying in the training of therapists, *Technique is what you use until the therapist arrives.* "Good methods can help a therapist find a way into the client's dilemma, but good therapy does not begin until the real-life therapist joins with the real life of the client."[6] Similarly, techniques in education help both novice and expert teachers assess the needs of learners and design appropriate instructional activities. However, the real teacher shows up when the techniques give way to human connections where both the teacher and student experience the vulnerability and excitement of the learning process.

If good teaching is more than technique, then high-quality professional development needs to include learning opportunities that meet teachers' needs beyond methods and skills. Parker Palmer argues that, "Good teaching can not be reduced to technique; good teaching comes from the identity and integrity of the teacher."[7] Good teachers and principals do not hide who they are. Their teaching and leadership express who they are. Each brings together a complex mix of experiences, social roles, and expectations in life and work. If, as Parker Palmer asserts, good teaching does flow from identity and integrity, how does professional development beyond work attend to strengthening the professional identity and integrity of teachers and principals? How do learning experiences that enhance these dimensions contribute to professional growth and enhanced professional practice? We begin with a definition of identity and integrity. Next, I describe essential features of professional development beyond work that attend to these important dimensions of professionalism.

Individual identity comes from a complex mix of personal experiences, interactions, and associations that make us who we are. Parker Palmer describes identity as, "a moving intersection of the inner and outer forces that make me who I am, converging in the irreducible mystery of being human."[8] Etienne Wenger links identity to negotiated meanings of experience that each of us has as members of various social communities, including communities of professional practice. How then does identity translate into real life?

My identity, for example, comes from the confluence of being a full professor at a midwestern research university, a white male of Norwegian descent, a husband, a guitar-playing grandfather, a church elder, and a gardener, to mention a few of the slices of social roles and experiences that make up the complex weave of my personal identity at the beginning of the 21st century. These bits of biography and experience shape my identity and help define who I am. They are inextricably embedded in my own learning and professional work.

The link between identity, community, and professional practice is an important one. In the formation of community, as well as in our professional practice, we each negotiate our identities. "This negotiation may be silent; participants may not necessarily talk directly about that issue. But whether or not they address the question directly, they deal with it through the way they engage in action with one another and relate to one another. Inevitably, our practices deal with the profound issue of how to be a human being."[9] What brings all of these aspects of identity together in ways that give meaning and purpose to one's life and work? Palmer provides an answer, "Integrity requires that I discern what is integral to my selfhood, what fits, and what does not—and that I choose life-giving ways of relating to the forces that converge within me."[10] Integrity is what gives distinctive shape and force to individual identity.

Integrity is not an inherited quality, but one that comes from active choices and reflection about one's own learning and life. Integrity involves a sense of wholeness and unity that is the product of bringing together the seemingly disparate patches of the crazy quilt of social interactions, roles, and diverse forces that shape who we are. Integrity lies not so much in bringing harmony and agreement to these forces but in finding ways that gives them meaning and purpose to life, even when some elements are contradictory. As a result, we reduce the fragmentation and separation of various aspects of our lives—personal, intellectual, professional, social, political, emotional, and spiritual. If good teaching and leadership practice are anchored in identity and integrity, then professional development "beyond" work provides pathways that nurture each and contribute to personal growth and enhanced professional practice. Next, we examine sources for nurturing and enriching the hearts, minds, and souls of educational professionals.

PROFESSIONAL DEVELOPMENT JOURNEYS "BEYOND" WORK

Earlier in this chapter, I defined professional development "beyond" work as experiences and learning opportunities away from school and not directly related to work that feed the heart, mind, soul, and passions of teachers and principals. This definition allows for at least two very different journeys. The first journey is one that literally goes beyond the boundaries of school and work to a vast array of individual and collective experiences that shape who teachers and principals are as people. The second is an inward journey that goes beyond the boundaries of daily work tasks to explore the inner landscapes of identity and meaning for teachers and principals.

Journeying Out There

We begin with the journey "out there"—experiences and occasions to learn and grow that are physically beyond schools and professional work. This may include such diverse experiences as individual hobbies, travel, community service projects, recreational pursuits, and alternative career explorations, to name a few. None is designed as a professional development, work-related experience, yet each becomes part of the constellation of lived experiences that forge links between individual identity, integrity, community, and professional work. In Chapter 1, I used the example of a trip to northern Sweden to illustrate what I meant by professional learning opportunities beyond work. How did this side-trip to a remote Sami encampment beyond the Arctic Circle in northern Sweden contribute to my own personal and professional growth?

Several years ago I was among a group of international scholars invited to Umea University to participate in a major conference for Swedish school administrators. This formal invitation, accompanied by requisite expectations for my participation in various parts of the conference, was my work assignment. Because formal presentations are an ordinary part of my professional work, what I have described to you thus far hardly merits much attention as an enriching professional development experience beyond work. The journey to the conference was such an experience.

Our Swedish host had invited presenters to a preconference visit to the northernmost school district in the world, Kiruna Kommun. Again, visiting a school district, albeit a unique and distant one, was still an ordinary part of my work. What made the visit such an enriching one was a journey to a Sami village, an educational trip beyond the school district, beyond the conference, and beyond my work. I use this personal experience to illustrate the possibilities and power in journeys beyond work that enhance professional thinking and practice.

The two-day preconference trip began with a four-hour culture sauna on the evening we arrived. It featured a banquet table of regional specialties, stout drinks, and periodic visits to the sauna, accompanied by local folk stories, and topped off with a welcomed night's sleep in the famous Ice Hotel at Jukkasjarvi. Vivid images come back to me with little effort—the chill of the frigid air in an exotic, ice-block room lavishly furnished with an ice-carved bed, furniture, and fixtures. The pungent smell of tanned reindeer hides on which we slept, and the welcoming aroma of hot lingonberry juice in the morning greeting me on my first day in the far north. The next day we traveled miles by snowmobile to a remote winter camp where we lassoed reindeer, competed in sled races, and feasted on fire-roasted reindeer, bread, and strong coffee under a tent of deerskins. The day was full of adventure and new experiences.

Notwithstanding the memorable personal experiences, the question remains: What does any of this have to do with professional development and work? I believe these experiences far beyond work have been woven into the fabric of my identity, integrity, sense of community, and professional work. I had been introduced to a unique culture with a worldview different from my own. For the Sami people we visited, the juxtaposition of centuries old traditions in a remote and primitive winter camp, complemented by cell phones and an occasional helicopter tour to check on the massive reindeer herd, represented contradictory, yet compatible, parts of their life north of the Arctic Circle. My assumptions and understandings about life and professional work in the modern world had been challenged. The dissonance created a tension that stretched my thinking and my being. For me, it was an enriching, transforming learning experience. The solitude and calm of life beyond the Arctic Circle made me wonder what had happened to these qualities in my own life, my work, and my teaching. Solitude and calm are truly endangered species in my world. Being connected to great traditions was another lesson from the north. The Sami enjoy a living history and culture that informs their daily lives while linking them to generations across the centuries. I too understand that I am part of a centuries old tradition—teaching and learning. This is especially important when educators are under attack accompanied by constant demands for accountability and exhortations to adopt the newest and latest ideas in the field. The journey was an example of expeditionary learning that reminded me once again of the importance of direct experience as an anchor for new learning and understanding. As I reflect on this visit, now two years past, the quality of "localness" also stands out. Despite being in a location far from cities and major intersections of cosmopolitan activities, there were rich and unique possibilities for learning and living. Last, the journey beyond rekindled a sense of wonder and awe, at times flooding my veins with the adrenalin rush that accompanies new ways of thinking, learning, and being.

Of course, not all lived experiences are occasions for professional learning and growth. John Dewey reminded us decades ago that not all experience is educative. Professional development "beyond" work is truly professionally educative when the experiences move us to reflect more deeply on the experience, our life, and work. These reflections become pathways to new insights and understandings integrated into the tapestry of living, learning, and work.

What role, if any, should schools take in sponsoring and encouraging such seemingly idiosyncratic, yet powerful learning opportunities? First, schools need to understand that the professional development is more than skills training. There are many life-enriching opportunities for teachers and principals that contribute to learning, growth, and improved professional practice. Second, schools can remove many of the traditional barriers in contracts, policies, and structures that limit growth beyond work. For example, school districts can make journeys beyond school and work possible through such mechanisms as leave policies for career and personal exploration (paid and unpaid), flexible contracts, and the creative use of time and daily work schedules.[11] Third, schools need to be more than passive gatekeepers to professional development beyond work. They can legitimize learning opportunities beyond work by providing information, encouraging participation, and developing opportunities in formal and informal venues for teachers to share their experiences with others.

The Journey Inward

Professional development beyond the traditional boundaries of work also includes inward journeys—beyond techniques and work tasks to deeper meanings and understandings of the connections among work, life, and learning. Parker Palmer suggests one route for this inward journey—the development of communities of professional discourse: places where teachers and principals talk about their work, but in ways well beyond surface conversations about activities and routine tasks. "If I want to teach well, it is essential that I explore my inner terrain. But I can get lost in there, practicing self-delusion and running in self-serving circles. So I need guidance that a community of collegial discourse provides—to say nothing of the support such a community can offer to sustain me in the trials of teaching and the cumulative and collective wisdom about this craft that can be found in every faculty worth its salt."[12] The journey inward is an opportunity for professional development beyond work.

The journey inward supports growth and development beyond work in at least three important ways. Deep reflection and conversation about teaching and learning go well beyond traditional exchanges among teachers and principals on methods and best practices. Exploring the inner terrains of teaching, living, and learning involves risk and opportunity in ways that workshops and traditional staff development activities rarely do. "Though technique-talk promises the 'practical' solutions that we think we want and need, the conversation is stunted when technique is the only topic: the human issues in teaching get ignored, so the human beings who teach feel ignored as well."[13] The journey inward attends to the human dimensions of teaching and leadership—its joys, frustrations, and uncertainties. The journey inward, supported by norms of individual and collective reflection and deep conversation, also builds connections among values, commitments, beliefs, and individual actions. These conversations give purpose and meaning to personal and professional lives. Last, the journey inward is not a solitary act; it is a journey supported by colleagues who share both the vulnerabilities and joys of teaching and learning. Given the importance of these inward journeys, what can schools do to support communities of practice that draw support and strength from deep conversations about teaching, living, and learning?

Professional learning communities support the journey inward for teachers and principals in a number of ways. Professional learning communities value conversations that explore the deeper interior landscapes of teaching and leadership. Learning communities have strong cultural norms that honor professional identity and meanings that link colleagues together in true communities of practice. Professional learning communities also find ways to create the time needed and occasions for deeper conversations about teaching. Staff retreats, structured study and discussion groups, and virtual networks connecting teachers in ongoing reflective conversations are three possibilities. The reflective interactions go beyond technique to explorations and new discoveries about the mysteries and complexities of teaching, learning, and being. Information gleaned from climate surveys, faculty handbooks, and orientation sessions at the start of the school year pales in comparison to these vivid descriptions of lived experience. Professional learning communities have leaders who do more than exhort others to journey inward; they show the way through personal example. These leaders are reflective and willing to expose their own vulnerabilities to others. Leaders also provide energy and direction when needed, and on occasion, enforce ground rules when individuals or groups violate collegial norms of trust and mutual respect.

It does not necessarily follow that because there is time and opportunity for the journey inward and for reflective conversations teachers and principals will naturally engage in those activities. In many schools, such conversations may be counternormative. Thus, in addition to time and opportunity, the journey inward requires changing the typical topics of conversations. However, changing the topic and nature of conversation is easier said than done. Leaders can support the journey inward by helping to redirect the topics of conversation. For instance, they might use such prompts as metaphors to describe professional work, paradoxes, dilemmas of practice, or critical incidents. Depending on the nature of group and setting, the following are ways to start conversation and the journey inward.

In reflective conversations, teachers and principals learn as much about themselves as they do about others. As they respond to various prompts and listen to the experiences of their colleagues, they gain perspective on their identities and their mutual interdependence in communities of practice. The journey inward needs an environment that encourages honest exchanges, maintains mutual respect, and establishes

Initiating Inward Journeys

- Describe a time when you knew that a particular student had really learned something and was excited about it because you could see it in the student's eyes.
- If learning was an animal and you were its caretaker, what animal would it be? Describe your role as its caretaker.
- Have you ever thought about quitting your job as a teacher? Principal? Tell us why. Why didn't you quit?
- If you had to chose one person who had the most influence on you becoming a teacher, who would it be? Tell us about him or her.
- Most of us have had mentors or significant people who influenced us early in our careers. Tell us about someone you remember. Why was he/she an important influence?
- Time and money are two of the most common responses given when teachers are asked to describe major obstacles to professional development in schools. If you were given a gift of 10 extra hours a week (not added to your work week but included in it), how would you use it?
- Describe your biggest disaster as a teacher or principal? What made it so bad? How did it make you feel? What did you learn from it?

ground rules that protect people as they explore these inner landscapes. Getting people to respond is important. Equally important is building individual and group capacity to listen—without judgment, quick answers, and facile solutions.

The conversations that emerge on the journey inward are sustained through dialogue. The capacity to listen and be part of a dialogue describes the dynamic process that, "allows us to be present to another person's problems in a quiet, receptive way that encourages the soul to come forth, a way that does not presume to know what is right for the other but allows the other's soul to find its own answers at its own level and pace. If we want to support each other's inner lives, we must remember a simple truth: the human soul does not want to be fixed, it wants simply to be seen and heard."[14] Teachers and principals develop the capacity to talk and listen to each other in ways that provide pathways to build joint understanding, create meaning, engender commitment, and provide opportunities to practice and enhance interactions and collective learning. Dialogue also helps teachers and principals deal with some of the common threats to collaborative learning and capacity building—defensiveness, ignoring or masking difficult issues, and the lack of deep and insightful analysis. "It is not the absence of defensiveness that characterizes learning teams, but the way defensiveness is faced. A team committed to learning must be committed not only to telling the truth about what going on 'out there' . . . and 'in here.'"[15]

CONCLUSION

Professional development beyond work does more than meet the minimum threshold of criteria that defines professional development. It acknowledges and highlights dimensions of teachers' and principals' personal and professional lives that have been ignored or marginalized in traditional professional development frameworks. Professional development beyond work describes two distinct journeys: journeys "out there" away from school and work and inward journeys that connect learning, living, and working. Both take teachers and principals beyond daily routines to vistas that give them new insights and deeper understandings of themselves as people and as professionals. Professional development beyond work complements the richness of learning opportunities "in," "at," and "outside" of work described in earlier chapters. Finally, professional development beyond work creates and celebrates the wholeness of teachers and principals by bringing together their inner and outer worlds of learning, work, and identity.

SITE VISITS

www.teacherformation.org
Homepage for The Courage to Teach Teacher Formation Center.
www.bbc.co.uk/dna/h2g2/A756047
The Ice Hotel in Jukkasjarvi, Sweden.
www.denverzoo.org/education/school_programs/teacher_programs/travel/
    travel.htm
A teacher travel program that gives you hands-on learning.
www.writingclasses.com
About Gotham Writers' Workshop Gotham Writers' Workshop is currently the largest private creative writing school in the United States. More than 80 faculty members teach the craft of writing to more than 4,000 students a year in New York City and online at WritingClasses.com. Classes include fiction writing, screenwriting, nonfiction writing, memoir writing, business writing, children's book writing, playwriting, novel writing, poetry writing, TV writing, comedy writing, film analysis, and reading fiction. Private instruction and workshops for young writers are also available.
www.ashburtoncentre.co.uk
The Ashburton Centre offers varied, exciting courses and holidays in Devon, UK, and Spain. These include specialist cooking courses run by Stella West-Harling as well as creative writing courses tutored by top writers.
www.habitat.org/
Habitat for Humanity
www.naesp.org/cgi-bin/netforum/teach/a/1
This is a job openings listing service for teaching jobs. It has been created by NAESP to be used at no cost to school districts and principals to post teaching positions and for teachers seeking jobs. Teachers may post resumes and their availability information.
www.irlgov.ie/edu/press/000928g.htm
Visiting Teacher Service

www.teachersatwork.com/
Teachers@Work is an innovative electronic employment service designed to match the professional staffing needs of schools with teacher applicants who can fill those positions. This nationwide, online database provides an efficient and economical way to overcome the geographical limitations of recruitment and reach the most desirable teaching candidates.
www.academploy.com
Academic Employment—educational employment from K-12 through university positions.
www.acpa.nche.edu
ACPA—online higher education job listings.
www.uaf.edu/atp/
Alaska Teacher Placement—teacher positions available in Alaska.
www.aacc.nche.edu
Careerline—community college employment job line.
chronicle.merit.edu/.ads/.links.html
Chronicle of Higher Education—higher education job listings.

SUPPLEMENTARY READING

Palmer, P. J. (1993). *To know as we are known*. San Francisco: Harper.
Palmer, P. J. (1998). *The courage to teach: Exploring the inner landscape of a teacher's life*. San Francisco: Jossey-Bass.
Wenger, E. (1998). *Communities of practice: Learning, meaning, and identity*. Cambridge, UK: Cambridge University Press.

NOTES

1. Palmer, P. J. (1998). *The courage to teach: Exploring the inner landscape of a teacher's life*. San Francisco: Jossey-Bass, 11.

2. Palmer, P. J. (1993). *To know as we are known*. San Francisco: Harper.

3. Ibid., 17.

4. Ibid., 11.

5. Ibid., 4.

6. Ibid., 5.

7. Ibid., 10.

8. Ibid., 13.

9. Wenger, E. (1998). *Communities of practice: Learning, meaning, and identity*. Cambridge, UK: Cambridge University Press.

10. Palmer, P. J. 13.

11. Bredeson, P. V. (2001). Negotiated learning: Union contracts and teacher professional development. *Educational Policy Analysis Archives, 9*(26). Retrieved July 1, 2002, from htpp://epaa.asu.edu/epaa/v9n26.htm

12. Palmer, P. J., 142.

13. Ibid., 145.

14. Ibid., 151.

15. Senge, P. (1990), *The fifth discipline: The art and practice of the learning organization.* New York: Currency Doubleday, 257.

Part III

Evaluating and Implementing New Designs for Professional Learning

9

Evaluating the Architecture of Professional Development

Architecture, then, stands at the intersection of societal need, available technology, and artistic theory.[1]

INTRODUCTION

The guiding metaphor for this book is architecture. In the first eight chapters, I have argued that professional development as architecture deals with the artful creation and use of learning spaces for teachers' and principals' growth and improvement. The architecture of professional development deals with the creation of learning opportunities that engage educators' creative and reflective capacities in ways that strengthen their practice. The purpose of this chapter is to provide guidelines for evaluating the new architecture for professional development. The chapter begins with a brief review of three essential architectural components presented in Chapter 1. Next, we examine how each architectural component is expressed in designs for professional learning and the implications for the evaluation of professional development. In the next section, I discuss considerations for assessing the design, delivery, content, context, and outcomes of professional development. In the fourth section, I describe three distinct contexts—political, organizational, and individual—for professional development evaluation. In the following section, I use a five-level evaluation framework for illustrating differences in purpose, value, methods, and utility assessing professional development "as," "in," "at," "outside of," and "beyond" work. The chapter concludes a model for constructing successful professional development evaluations.

UTILITAS, FIRMITAS, AND VENUSTAS: A REPRISE

In Chapter 1, citing the contemporary work of James O'Gorman and the classic works of ancient Roman architect Vitruvius, I described three essential components in architecture—utilitas (function), firmitas (structure), and venustas (beauty). See Figure 1.1. In the chapters that followed, we examined how each of these essential components is expressed in designs for professional learning. Though we may use somewhat different language today to describe the essentials of architecture, the three components resonate with the principles of effective professional development described in current literature. The idea that form follows function is as true in designs for professional learning as it is for buildings. Utilitas (function) means that the priorities, interests, and needs of clients determine the design, context, content, and delivery of professional development. Understanding what clients want and need depends a great deal on who is identified as a client of professional development. Clearly, teachers and administrators are the most obvious clients. However, designs for staff development that give attention to the needs and interests of students, local policy makers (reflecting districts goals and school improvement plans), and community stakeholders are far more likely to be successful in terms of impact and sustainability than ones that consider only the participants in training and development activities.

The second component is firmitas (structure). Structure includes the materials, processes, and organizational features used to create and sustain opportunities for learning "in," "at," "outside," and "beyond" work that address the interests, needs, and priorities of clients. Elements of structure include adequate time (within and beyond educators' workdays) for study, for consultation, and for reflection to deepen learning and transfer new learning into practice. Designs for professional learning anchored in principles of cognition, expert knowledge, and human and organizational development require appropriate materials, conditions, and resources (financial, political, and personnel).

The third essential component of architecture is venustas (beauty). This aesthetic element comes from the artistic arrangement and use of design, delivery, content, and context to create learning spaces that engage

Sara's Poster

Sara stands beside her trifold poster during a class session where teachers and administrators are sharing the results of their action research projects. She is excited to talk with her colleagues about what she has been doing over the past semester. The poster is a window into Sara's questions about her professional work, her learning journey through action research, and her plans to improve her teaching practice. The visual images highlight key findings from her inquiry, reflections on her work, and how this professional development activity influenced her thinking and work as a teacher. The poster represents the artful arrangement of time for study, consultation, and reflection; appropriate materials, conditions, and resources; and support people to assist her along the way. Sara's commitment and passion for excellence in teaching displayed in this poster session is truly a thing of beauty.

The Fall Retreat

After 10 years of faculty retreats, one fall retreat ended with more energy and possibility than anyone thought possible. Like retreats in the past, there was a plan, the resources were available, and we were all there. But somehow this retreat was different from the outset. With the arrival of three newly hired faculty members, we were excited about our future. We listened more carefully to one another. We built on each other's ideas. We revised the plan for the day when the agenda threatened to separate us into small work groups. We wanted to talk, listen, and be together as a team. We felt valued and believed in our collective strengths. The day was charged with enthusiasm and synergy. The sense of shared purpose and accomplishment at day's end felt good! The successful welcoming of new colleagues, wrestling with big ideas and new challenges, rethinking our programs, and working and learning together in a dynamic, aesthetic interaction was the hoped-for result of careful planning and sturdy structure. It was truly an artful performance of team learning. The fall retreat brought together the essential components of professional development architecture—function, structure, and beauty.

teachers and administrators in learning opportunities that meet their needs and change them as people and professionals. As a reader you may still have your doubts about the aesthetics of professional development; to address those doubts, I use two concrete examples to illustrate what I mean by beauty in professional development.

The work of architects for professional development is to create artful designs for learning (venustas) with structural integrity (firmitas) that appropriately meet the needs of teachers, administrators, and the students and communities they serve (utilitas). Thus, the assessment of professional development requires an evaluation that goes well beyond simple satisfaction surveys given to participants. The evaluation of professional development consists of the systematic collection and analysis of data to examine the impact of learning activities on teachers, students, schools, and professional communities.

WHY EVALUATE PROFESSIONAL DEVELOPMENT?

Before we consider the "what" and "how" of professional development evaluations, it is important that we consider "why" we evaluate professional development. There are at least seven reasons for the growing interest in evaluation of professional development.

- Return on Investment—Researchers have estimated that the direct and indirect costs of professional development in schools costs approximately $19 billion annually.[2] To paraphrase Everett Dirksen, former U.S. senator from Illinois, "a billion here and billion there, and soon you're talking about real money." It is reasonable to assume that taxpayers, policy makers, and practitioners have a vested interest in finding out whether or not they are getting any return on their substantial investment of money, time, and materials in professional development for teachers and administrators.

- Better Information for Planning—Policy makers, as well as participants and providers of professional development, need better information to guide their decisions and choices in the design, delivery, content, context, and intended outcomes of professional development. Being able to provide reliable and valid data on various dimensions of professional development through systematic evaluation is especially critical with greater demands for accountability.

- Professional Development and School Improvement—Professional learning is at the heart of school improvement and educational reform. Evaluation of professional development is important because both practitioners and policy makers want a better understanding of how people learn, develop expertise, change their practice, and ultimately influence student learning.

- Linking Professional Development to Cognitive Science—Linking professional development evaluation to what we know from cognitive science, provides strong evidence that teachers and administrators, like all learners, bring distinct prior learning and experiences to new learning and they have different learning styles. Evaluations, especially assessments that provide valuable diagnostic information on learner needs, interests, and learning style preferences, are critical to planning and designing effective learning opportunities for teachers and administrators.

- Evaluating the Validity of Professional Development—There is no shortage of lists that describe the characteristics/features of what good professional development is.[3] Evaluation is a systematic means for gathering and analyzing data to assess the validity of these taxonomies. Further, evaluation will help address a number of issues related to the "goodness" of professional development. Good for what? Good for whom? Good under what conditions?

- Professional Learning and Changes in Practice—The shift in education toward the assessment of educational outcomes, especially what students know and are able to do, bolstered by standards-based reform initiatives, is also a major force behind the growing interest in evaluation of teacher and administrator professional learning outcomes. What participants in professional development need to know and be able to do, as well as the impact of those learning outcomes, logically follows from the shift toward greater attention on outcomes over inputs.

- Professional Learning and Compensation—Last, a number of local school districts and states are experimenting with alternative compensation systems for teacher pay.[4] The legitimacy and equity of alternative compensation systems anchored in reliable and valid measures of professional knowledge, skills, and performance requires careful attention to the evaluation of professional development and its outcomes. The allocation of resources to support some types of training and development and not others provides further evidence that system rewards and professional learning are being linked in terms of policy and practice.

EVALUATING PROFESSIONAL DEVELOPMENT: PURPOSES AND CONTEXTS

Before we can design an evaluation process that meets commonly accepted standards for effective assessment,[5] we need to address some basic questions. These include: What do we want to know? Why is this information important? How can we gather and analyze data to address these questions? How will these evaluation data be used? Responses to these questions suggest two major dimensions for the planning stages of the evaluation of professional development: the *purposes* of the evaluation; and the *contexts of use* of the evaluation.

Citing the works of evaluation experts, Tom Guskey notes that regardless of the evaluation model employed there are three general purposes for evaluation. These include assessments done for the purposes of:

(a) planning; (b) monitoring/adjusting/improving programs and processes (formative); and (c) making judgments and decisions based on the program's overall quality and impact (summative). "Most evaluations are actually designed to fulfill all three of these purposes, although the emphasis on each changes during various stages of the evaluation process."[6] I recognize the overlaps and interdependencies among the three purposes for evaluation; however, in this section I separate them deliberately to sharpen important distinctions that influence the design of professional development evaluation processes.

In addition to understanding the purposes of evaluation, it is also important to understand the contexts of use for evaluation data. There are three important contexts to consider in the evaluation of professional development. The *policy context* consists of legislative bodies, educational agencies (federal, state, and regional), and local school boards whose decisions influence nearly all aspects of schooling, including professional development. Evaluation information provided within the policy context influences decisions regarding the focus, funding, and forms of professional development. One recent example of evaluation research that informs policy choices is *Designing Effective Professional Development: Lessons from the Eisenhower Program.*[7] The *organizational context* refers to school and district levels where local discussions, decisions, and implementation strategies are carried out. At the school and district levels, where resources (time, money, and personnel) are often scarce, information on the efficacy and impact of locally sponsored professional development helps teachers and administrators make choices on the allocation of resources to support professional learning (individual and collective) aligned with district goals and local school improvement priorities. The third context of use is in the hot action of *practice*, where individual teachers or teams translate what they know into practices that support student learning and development.[8] Each context of use represents distinct combinations of needs, interests, priorities, and responsibilities. The evaluation purposes and interests of state legislators and federal education officials are likely to differ substantially from those of local school board members and classroom teachers. The intersection of evaluation *purposes* (planning, monitoring, and decision making) and the distinct *contexts of use* (policy, organization, and practice) helps evaluators address basic questions as they design and carry out assessments of the design, delivery, content, context, and outcomes of professional development.

CRITICAL LEVELS OF PROFESSIONAL DEVELOPMENT EVALUATION

Evaluating the outcomes of professional development has confounded researchers and practitioners for decades. In most school districts, the lack of reliable and valid assessment tools, personnel, and resources to support the systematic evaluation of professional development has resulted in assessments that are little more than simple satisfaction measures and compliance exercises. The paucity of empirical evidence on the effectiveness of professional development, however, has not dissuaded school districts from investing billions of dollars annually to enhance the professional knowledge and skills of teachers and school administrators in the belief that the investment contributes significantly to teacher learning and change, school improvement, and enhanced student learning outcomes.

In a sustained effort to address limitations in professional development evaluation, Tom Guskey identified five critical levels for the assessment of professional development. His five-level model is hierarchically arranged from simple to more complex assessments, with higher levels requiring more resources, that is, time, money, and measurement expertise, and building on the successful evaluations at earlier levels.[9] At Level I, evaluators are interested in participants' reactions to the learning experience. Most of us are very familiar with postworkshop evaluations that ask us what we liked or did not like about various aspects of the professional development activity. At Level II, the assessment focuses on indicators of participant learning—new knowledge and skills for example. Assessments at Level III focus on indicators of organizational support and change. The former examines aspects of context and process that support professional development while the latter looks at the impact of professional development on the organization. At Level IV, evaluators are interested in knowing if and how participants use their newly acquired knowledge and skills in practice. At Level V, the focus is on student learning outcomes resulting from professional development.

Guskey's five-level model is particularly helpful as we consider the evaluation of the new architecture of professional development. Figure 9.1 displays the intersection of the five critical levels of evaluation (participants' reactions, participants' learning, organizational support and change, participants' use of new knowledge/skills, and student learning outcomes) with four professional learning venues (professional development "in," "at," "outside," and "beyond" work). To illustrate, I use professional learning experiences described in earlier chapters. Four key questions guide the design of professional development evaluations to assess each learning experience.

1. Purpose—what do we want to know?
2. Value—why is the evaluation information important?
3. Methods—how will we gather and analyze evaluation data?
4. Utility—how will the evaluation data be used?

Participants' Reactions: Journey to a Sami Camp

My recent visit to a Sami camp in the Arctic region of northern Sweden was a professional development journey beyond work. What might a

Figure 9.1   Critical Levels of Professional Development Evaluation

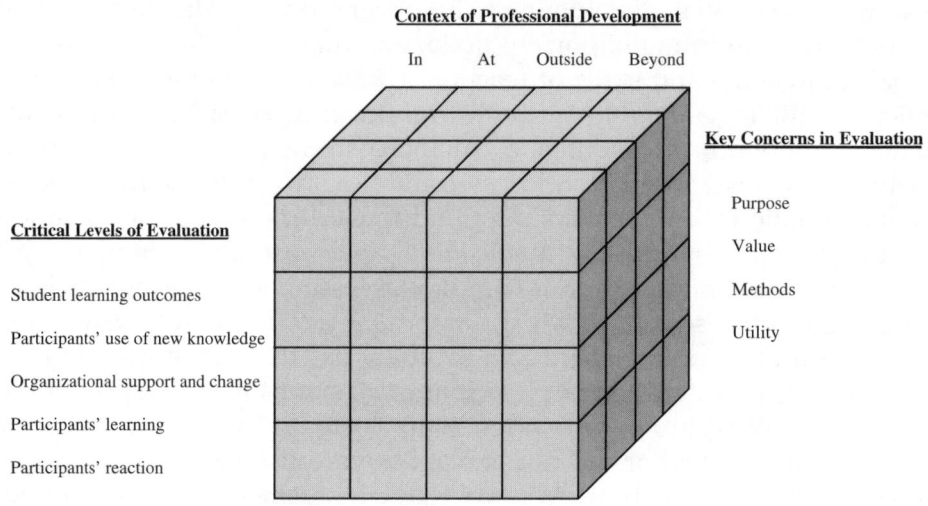

level-one evaluation of participants' reactions look like? A major purpose of such an evaluation is to become aware of unique personal learning experiences and to understand individual reactions to them. For instance, we might want to ask: What was it like to be in a Sami camp? What surprised you about the day? What are the most memorable parts of this journey? The value of this evaluation is to better understand the potential of learning experiences beyond work and their influence on teachers' personal and professional growth. Written reflections in logs and professional development plans, formal presentations, and reflective interviews with colleagues are possible methods for gathering, analyzing, and understanding participants' reactions to such experiences. A participant's reaction evaluation has utility because it honors the lived experiences of individuals and it has the potential to stimulate others to explore the learning rich terrains beyond school.

Participants' Learning: Classroom Action Research

Action research is an example of professional development in work embedded in teachers' daily instructional routines. Teachers and administrators systematically gather, analyze, interpret, and adjust their actions around a particular aspect of their professional work. What are some possibilities for evaluating learning through action research? The purpose of this evaluation is to understand what teachers learn as they carry out classroom action research studies, or what principals learn about their leadership and its effects on others and on school improvement. Questions might include: What did you set out to learn? What did you learn about your teaching? Your leadership? Have you acquired any new knowledge or skills during your action research project? Assessing what and how much teachers and principals learn while conducting action research is valuable to both policy makers and participants who have an interest in knowing whether or not the time and resources required to conduct action research is worth the investment. Authentic methods for educators to track and reflect on their learning include: written logs where practitioner researchers reflect on what they learn and how they learn; and visual creations and representations on a trifold poster where they summarize action research findings and action plans. How might evaluation information on teacher learning through action research be used? Knowing what and how much teachers and principals learned has utility because it helps address questions regarding cost and benefits of this type of work-embedded learning. Also, these evaluation data help in pre-assessment phases of professional development planning and in the design and delivery of suitable content for ongoing action research skills training and implementation.

Organizational Support and Change: Peer Coaching

In a level-three evaluation, the purpose is to assess the context and the impact of professional development experiences. Evaluation questions concerning context may include: Are there adequate resources, materials, and trained personnel to effectively implement peer coaching? In what way(s) do current school structures and processes support or hinder effective peer coaching? Evaluation of organizational support and change also includes an assessment of the impact of peer coaching. We would want to know, for instance, if peer coaching affected the school's climate, cultural norms, the nature of teacher work, and communication patterns among teachers. Assessing the context and impact of peer coaching provides valuable information for judging the implementation and quality of peer coaching opportunities in schools and its contributions to individual, group, and school capacities. Proponents of peer coaching argue that colleague observations, consultations, professional dialogue, and collaborative work do more than benefit individual participants. These professional development activities "at" work build norms of professional community, deepen teacher talk and thinking about teaching and learning, and contribute significantly to organizational change and improvement processes. School climate surveys, focus group interviews, and participant portfolios are among the methods teachers use to systematically gather and analyze data on the context and impact of peer coaching in their school. Finally, these evaluation data have utility. Teachers and administrators can use these data as they develop school improvement plans, work to create norms of interdependent collegiality, and improve the classroom instructional practices that enhance student learning.

Participants' Use of New Knowledge and Skills: Off-Site Technology Training

A common professional development experience for teachers is off-site training in workshops. In fact, the one-day workshop has been the proverbial "workhorse" of staff development. Yet, our experiences and the work of cognitive psychologists remind us that the transfer of new knowledge and skills from one setting to another is not automatic, nor always successful. Thus, the purpose for evaluation of participants' use of newly gained technology skills is to determine the degree to which these skills are put to use in their daily professional practice. This level of evaluation also helps us identify any problems the teacher may be having using technology skills (e.g., Web-based information searches) in teaching. The value of participants' use of new knowledge is to understand concerns and issues around transfer of learning and successful implementation of new teaching and learning strategies in classrooms. Three methods to gather information on participants' use of new technology skills include the use of surveys, written questionnaires, or interviews to ask teachers such questions as: How frequently do you use Web-based resource searches in your classes? What types of teaching activities and content seem most amenable to using these skills? What problems have you encountered trying to use new technology skills in your teaching? Evaluating the transfer of new technology skills enables schools to determine the types of on-site personnel support and expertise needed for effective implementation in classrooms. The information generated from participants' use of new skills is helpful (utility) for: assessing transfer of learning; determining types of on-site resources (personnel, time, and expertise) needed for effective implementation in classrooms; anticipating problems; and planning for future off-site training experiences.

Student Learning Outcomes: Teacher Study Groups

The primary aim of staff development is to enhance teachers' and administrators' knowledge and skills to strengthen their practice. Though laudable, and even altruistic, the bottom line for investing resources in teacher and administrator personal and professional development is the enhancement of student learning—cognitive, emotional, and psychomotor. Examining the relationships among training experiences, teacher learning, teacher instructional practices, and student learning is a complex evaluation task. Despite its challenges, the purpose of level-five evaluation is to understand the ways in which teacher learning "in," "at," "outside of," and "beyond" work affects student learning. To illustrate the complexity of such an assessment, as well as to suggest possibilities, let us use a professional development "at work" experience, teacher study groups.

Teacher study groups are an example of collaborative learning in professional learning communities. Because study groups frequently take place in schools, there are several natural advantages to this type of professional learning experience. The topics and concerns are generally teacher generated so there is commitment on the part of teachers. Also, because study group learning is *in situ*, transfer of learning problems is mitigated. Evaluating the impact of these study groups on student learning is valuable because it provides teachers and administrators with the most convincing evidence that collaborative learning among teachers is a synergistic force for school improvement and enhanced student learning. Collaborative action research is a particularly effective method for evaluating the connections between teacher collaborative learning in study groups and student outcomes. Teacher reflections and data in electronic portfolios, surveys of parents, students, and administrators, and a wide range of student outcome measures (standardized test scores, attitudinal measures, and student work/performances) are among the sources of evaluation data for evaluating the impact of professional development on student learning. Evaluation data generated in action research teams becomes valuable feedback for teachers as they consider their learning, their instructional practices, and their students' learning.

Perhaps the most obvious implication of the matrix for professional development evaluation displayed in Figure 9.1 is that there is no such thing as a generic evaluation for professional learning. Credible evaluations are not the same as rigorous assessment instruments and tools. High-quality evaluation is the product of appropriate use of assessment instruments combined with adequate resources to address particular questions of interest in professional development policies, programs, or practices. Gathering evidence about teachers' immediate reactions to an in-school training session has utility. However, the information gathered in such an assessment is much more valuable in terms of judging the quality of the design and delivery of particular learning experiences than it is in providing useful information describing the degree to which new learning is put into practice in teachers' classrooms.

CONSTRUCTING SUCCESSFUL PROFESSIONAL DEVELOPMENT EVALUATIONS

An underlying proposition of Guskey's model for professional development evaluation is that higher levels of evaluation are built on successful evaluations at lower levels. These successes are scaffolds for more complex and refined assessments of professional learning and its outcomes. What factors contribute to successful evaluations? Figure 9.2 identifies five key elements that support successful professional development evaluation. Successful evaluation requires a clear, client-centered purpose; adequate support capacity (time, money, institutional structures and processes, materials, and committed/expert personnel); reliable and credible methods for

Figure 9.2 Key Elements for Successful Evaluation of Professional Development

Clear purpose	Adequate resources	Appropriate methods	Feasibility	Plan for use		Impact of evaluation
Clear Purpose	Adequate resources	Methods	Feasibility	Plan for use	=	Successful evaluation linking professional learning and school goals
	Adequate resources	Methods	Feasibility	Plan for use	=	Fragmented and confusing assessments
Clear Purpose		Methods	Feasibility	Plan for use	=	Limited and superficial assessments
Clear Purpose	Adequate resources		Feasibility	Plan for use	=	Invalid data and potential conflict
Clear Purpose	Adequate resources	Methods		Plan for use	=	Wasted resources and discredited evaluation
Clear Purpose	Adequate resources	Methods	Feasibility		=	Little impact on learning and future professional development

gathering and analyzing evaluation data; feasibility within the school/ district's resource, context, and political realities; and a plan for using the evaluation data that aligns with school improvement goals and supports professional learning and student learning. The figure also suggests problems that emerge when key elements are missing.

CONCLUSION

The evaluation of professional development is a critical part of school improvement planning. When evaluations are planned carefully and are successfully implemented in schools, they yield vital information for strengthening professional learning communities. Successful professional development evaluations do not create learning communities; they merely reveal their essence. The new architecture of professional development expressed in professional learning communities brings together three essential design components—utilitas, firmitas, and venustas. Evaluation of professional development serves three critical purposes in schools. First, the assessment of professional development provides valuable information for planning and goal setting. Second, evaluation guides organizational improvement processes. Third, evaluation of professional learning addresses important questions regarding the value of significant investments of resources (time, money, and personnel) in professional development in education.

In Chapter 10, we turn our attention to a discussion of how to move the creative energies and ideas of the new architecture for professional development from the design studio into schools. Specifically, I describe ways to use design principles of the new architecture for professional development to create learning spaces for teachers and principals.

SITE VISITS

www.ncrel.org/pd/

The North Central Regional Educational Laboratory contains resources and materials to support assessment of professional development. See especially the online version of Professional Development: Learning from the best: A toolkit for schools and districts based on the National Awards Program for Model Professional Development.

http://nsdc.org/

The National Staff Development Council Web site contains standards and assessment tools for examining content, context, and processes of professional development.

www.ascd.org

Association for Supervision and Curriculum Development Web site provides listings of resources and materials for evaluation of professional development.

SUPPLEMENTARY READING

Danielson, C., & McGreal, T. L. (2000). *Teacher evaluation to enhance professional practice*. Alexandria, VA: Association for Supervision and Curriculum Development.

Glatthorn, A. A., & Fox, L. E. (1996). *Quality teaching through professional development*. Thousand Oaks, CA: Corwin Press.

Guskey, T. R. (2000). *Evaluating professional development*. Thousand Oaks, CA: Corwin Press.

U.S. Department of Education. (1999). *Designing effective professional development: Lessons from the Eisenhower Program*. Washington, DC: Author.

NOTES

1. O'Gorman, J. F. (1998). *ABC of architecture*. Philadelphia: University of Pennsylvania Press,. 16.

2. Corcoran, T. C. (1995). *Transforming professional development for teachers: A guide for state policymakers*. Washington, DC: National Governors' Association; Bredeson, P. V. (1996). *Teachers take charge of their learning*. Washington, DC: National Foundation for the Improvement of Education.

3. See, for example, reports from the National Staff Development Council, U.S. Department of Education, and NCREL.

4. Odden, A., & Kelley, C. (1996). *Paying teachers for what they know and can do*. Thousand Oaks, CA: Corwin Press.

5. Joint Committee on Standards for Educational Evaluation. (1994*). The program evaluation standards* (2nd ed.). Newbury Park, CA: Sage Publications.

6. Guskey, T. (2000). *Evaluating professional development*. Thousand Oaks, CA: Corwin Press, 56.

7. Garet, M. S., Birman, B., Porter, A., Desimone, L., Herman, R., & Suk Yoon, K. (1999). *Designing effective professional development: Lessons from the Eisenhower Program*. Washington, DC: U.S. Department of Education.

8. Eraut, M. (1994). *Developing professional knowledge and competence*. London: Falmer Press.

9. Guskey, T. (2000). *Evaluating professional development*.

10

From Design Studio to School Site

Architecture can go beyond speechless beauty; it can communicate like any other language.[1]

INTRODUCTION

Like its artistic counterpart, the architecture of professional development deals with the creation of learning spaces using appropriate materials and structures that are useful, and when artfully done, even beautiful. The creative design of learning opportunities for teachers and principals is the essence of professional development. The chapter begins with a survey of the landscape of professional development. I review the major themes developed in each of the first nine chapters. In the second section, I describe some of the challenges that confront policy makers and practitioners as they work to move the new architecture for professional development from the design studio to school sites and into educators' personal and professional lives. Confronting these challenges requires rethinking, restructuring, and reculturing the spaces for professional learning in education. The chapter ends with a discussion of the messages and meaning communicated in the new architecture for professional development.

REVIEWING THE LANDSCAPE OF PROFESSIONAL DEVELOPMENT

Breaking the Box: New Designs for Professional Learning in Schools

At the end of the 19th century, Frank Lloyd Wright reconsidered the basic design and structure of the American house. The new architecture that emerged from his desire to create living spaces that harmonized natural and man-made environments expressed his belief that the ideals and spirit of a free people in a democratic society should be reflected in the way and in the places they live. His vision transformed architecture. At the beginning of the 21st century, professional development requires a similar transformation; it requires a new architecture that reflects our collective values and beliefs about learning, professionalism, and education in a democratic society. Breaking the mold of traditional staff development requires rethinking, restructuring, and reculturing designs for professional learning in schools and beyond. The new architecture of professional development reconsiders the design, delivery, content, context, and outcomes of professional learning. Changing the paradigm for professional development in education requires a clear vision, requisite knowledge and skills, appropriate resources and incentive structures, and a building plan for creating learning spaces for teachers and principals.

Building Beneath the Surface: Footings and Foundations in Professional Development

Like physical structures, footings and foundations support the designs for professional learning in schools. These foundations need to be *wide enough* to withstand periodic upheavals caused by severe conditions affecting the site; *deep enough* to distribute the weight and pressures on professional learning structures and processes; and *durable enough* to hold up over time. Specifications for laying these foundations are a function of the unique mix of local history, school culture, organizational priorities, community environment, and available resources. Building foundations beneath the surface to support new designs for professional learning requires four critical levels of action—personal, structural, political, and cultural.

Another important part of the foundation is a clear definition of professional development. Professional development refers to learning opportunities that engage educators' creative and reflective capacities in ways that strengthen their practice. This definition is anchored in three important concepts. First, professional development must be an occasion for learning. Second, the learning experience needs to engage teachers' and administrators' creative and reflective capacities as professionals. And third, though there are a number of desirable outcomes from professional development, the primary purpose of professional development is to strengthen practice.

Creating a Professional Learning Community

Every year schools invest billions of dollars in professional development believing that creating learning-enriched environments for teachers and principals will enhance professional practice and increase student-learning outcomes. The creation of professional learning communities (PLC) has become an important educational reform initiative across the United States. In an authentic PLC, teachers and administrators share a deep understanding of the meaning, responsibilities, expectations, and commitments embodied in three core concepts—*professional*, *learning*, and *community*. The principal building blocks for creating these learning communities are a clear and focused mission; a coherent instructional program supported by professional development, a strong professional culture, and appropriate decision-making structures; an accountability system linking goals, processes, and desired learning outcomes; and strong leadership.

Professional learning communities are also characterized by their ability to deal with the paradox of learning and unlearning. In the process of becoming authentic professional learning communities, schools and the people in them develop their individual and collective capacities to systematically unlearn (abandon) unproductive or outmoded structures, processes, practices, and ways of thinking.

Professional Development "As" Work

The current prominence of professional development in various educational reform initiatives masks the uncertain, and sometimes marginalized, status it has enjoyed historically in education. In fact, one scholar referred to professional development as an educational "stepchild" while others reported that its reputation was sullied because it was inefficient, ineffective, and generally poorly implemented. On a deeper level, I believe this reputation comes from the failure to see professional development as legitimate work. However unintended, when inservice training days, workshops, and study leaves are referred to as *something other than work*, or *an add-on to work*, or, worse, *time off from work*, professional development is diminished. The new architecture of professional development represents an expanded view of professional learning and practice. Moving professional development from the margins of professional work to its core has significant implications for teachers, administrators, and school boards as they work together to create a new architecture for professional learning in their schools.

Professional Development "In" Work

Professional development "in" work refers to the rich variety of learning opportunities embedded in the daily work of teachers and principals. Their professional work provides continuous opportunities for them to gain new knowledge, practice and refine skills, deepen insights on teaching and learning, and reflect on those learning experiences all while carrying out their primary work. Learning is inextricably embedded in the work itself. Using a two-by-two matrix, learning opportunities "in" work are categorized into four general types based on structure (informal or formal) and whether the learning experience is individual or collaborative. Examples of each include *individual informal* (reading, reflection-in-teaching); *individual structured* (classroom action research, creating a portfolio); *collaborative informal* (teacher talk, interactions on projects); and *collaborative structured* (peer coaching, team teaching).

Professional Development "At" Work

Professional development "at" work (workplace learning) refers to on-site learning opportunities for teachers that occur at times during the school day when they are not working directly with students or preparing to teach. Inservice training, workshops, meetings, and in-school exchanges are examples of workplace learning opportunities in schools. Professional development "at" work has obvious advantages: the efficient use of resources; the facilitated transfer of learning; the accommodation of different needs and learning styles; the ability to tap the collective knowledge and expertise of the staff; and the tendency to naturally promote collaboration, professional interdependence, and school renewal. While these advantages are important, there are also potential problems in workplace learning. It is possible that not all learning "at" work is good. For example, learning outcomes might include negative lessons learned; reinforcement of existing biases and the status quo; refinement of poor practices and habits; and learning outcomes unconnected to school priorities and student needs. In professional learning communities, teachers and principals find ways to create optimal conditions that support professional learning "at" work while mitigating any potential negative learning outcomes.

Professional Development "Outside" of Work

Teachers and principals have always enjoyed a wide variety of professional learning opportunities "outside of" work. Conventions, visits to other schools, summer institutes, university courses, and study leaves are examples of off-site professional development opportunities. Because many of these learning experiences are individual ones, team learning is critical to building collective capacity. Successful schools develop strategies to share knowledge, skills, and wisdom from individual experiences outside of work. Successful schools employ a systems thinking approach to align the energies and resources across professional development design, delivery, content, context, and outcomes of professional development "outside of" work maximizing individual learning while building organizational capacity.

Professional Development "Beyond" Work

Professional development beyond work refers to various enriching life experiences and learning opportunities that are away from work and school, ones that do not relate directly to practice. These learning and growth experiences feed the heart, mind, soul, and passions of teachers and principals. They also acknowledge two dimensions of teachers' and principals' personal and professional lives, identity and integrity, that are often ignored in traditional professional development frameworks. Professional development "beyond" work describes two types of journeys. The first is one is a journey *out there*, far beyond schools and work. The second is an inward journey connecting work, life, and learning. Both take teachers and principals beyond their daily routines to vistas that give them new insights and deeper understandings of themselves, their work, and the world in which they live.

Evaluating the Architecture of Professional Development

Assessing the quality and impact of teachers' and principals' professional development experience has become increasingly important for educational planning, program improvement, and decision making at all levels of educational governance. Understanding the context and purpose of these assessments guides evaluators' choices concerning the focus, methods, and use of these evaluation data. Using Guskey's five critical levels of evaluation (participant reaction, participant learning, participant use of knowledge and skills, organizational change and support, and student learning outcomes) a matrix is presented to illustrate how each level addresses four key concerns—*purpose*, *value*, *methods*, and *utility*. Effective evaluation of the new architecture of professional development provides critical information for the designers, participants, and supporters of professional learning communities.

CONFRONTING CHALLENGES IN DESIGNS FOR PROFESSIONAL LEARNING

Moving the new architecture for professional development into schools faces a number of challenges. To begin, there are powerful traditions and professional norms that may initially resist attempts to redesign professional learning opportunities in schools. Negative experiences that many educators have had with traditional staff development have left them wary, and sometimes cynical, about new possibilities for professional learning. They wonder, Will the new architecture really be different? Or, will it simply be a disguised version of earlier top-down, imposed requirements? Developing professional and cultural norms that teachers and principals are in charge of their professional development will take time, trust, and no small measure of individual and institutional tenacity.

A second challenge for the new architecture of professional development is the condition of the site. In a few cases, the individual school site may be open and ready for new ideas and new plans for professional learning and growth. In most, however, there are existing structures, practices, and beliefs that will need attention. In these cases, the debris will need to be cleared away, perhaps through strategic abandonment exercises or educational garage sales. In other situations, the materials and resources from former structures will be recycled and used to build new designs for professional learning.

There are two paradoxes that also present challenges to the new architecture for professional development. The new architecture represents both defined and unbounded learning spaces. Architecture as a creative process defines and encloses space using appropriate materials and structures to meet specific needs. Defining professional learning spaces "in" and "beyond" schools gives form to new designs for professional development. However, the creation of space does not limit the possible styles and opportunities for professional learning and growth. The design principles for a new architecture give form and opportunity for matching professional learning opportunities with individual needs and school sites.

Consequently, there is no *best* model or *best* practice for professional development. Clearly, there are a number of common characteristics and features of effective professional development. However, this does not mean there is one set of design specifications and formulaic processes and activities for professional learning. For readers who were searching for right answers, sure-fire models, and best practices in professional development, they are likely quite disappointed about not finding them in this book. I remain suspicious of the term, *best practice*, commonly used in the educational literature. "Best" is a superlative implying that one practice is the most effective practice. Given the uniqueness of teacher and school needs, school context and culture, personnel, and the types and amount of resources available, the idea that there is one *best* practice that matches highly diverse and dynamic school conditions across 15,000 school districts is unlikely. To be sure, there is much to be learned from the successes of others. However, simple imitation and replication of activities designed for teachers' and principals' professional learning needs in an urban setting will not necessarily match those in a small rural school. The new architecture of professional development is about developing practices and norms for continuous, enriching learning experiences for educational professionals; it is not about building a temple to best practice in professional development.

A second paradox for designers using the principles of the new architecture for professional development comes from the desire to create professional learning opportunities that are both enduring and changeable. How can designs for professional development be stable and flexible structures? In Chapter 2, I described the importance of building beneath the surface. Establishing a foundation that gives support, stability, and consistency to professional development practices over time is critical. I return to the work of Frank Lloyd Wright to suggest a way of dealing with this important contradiction in the architecture of professional development.

Taliesin was Wright's home as well as a working model for various design innovations. He viewed this hilltop complex as an ongoing architectural experiment, not a permanently fixed one. Consequently, he often neglected to lay deep footers. History leaves us with a working experiment frozen in time. Today, what stands as a monument to Wright's creative architectural genius is a structure threatened by ravages of climate, soil shifts, and water damage. Taliesin was viewed as an organic, yet enduring structure. Wright's design features and basic materials, stone and timbers, gave it a feeling of permanence and sturdiness. Nonetheless, sections of the house were redesigned and rebuilt several times. Other sections were removed. Materials used in one section of the house later reappeared in new parts of the house. I would argue that the new architecture for professional development is also a working model for learning, living, and working in schools. Familiar staff development activities, old materials, and new resources will be arranged in new ways to meet the ongoing professional development needs of teachers and principals. Finding the right mix of sturdiness and flexibility for creating professional learning communities is a significant challenge.

Finally, moving the new architecture from the design studio into schools requires three major shifts in schools—rethinking, restructuring, and reculturing professional development. This is no small task. This three-pronged approach represents a major systemic change in education. We know from experience in managing complex change that creating a new architecture for professional development in schools requires a clear vision, appropriate knowledge and skills, adequate resources, meaningful incentives, and a plan to get us there.

THE LANGUAGE OF ARCHITECTURE

The new architecture for professional development represents a set of design principles and structures for creating learning spaces for teachers and principals. Architecture is also a language. The styles, shapes, and spaces of buildings, monuments, and new designs for professional learning in schools send messages. Let us reflect for a moment on the language of the new architecture for professional development. What messages does the new architecture for professional development send? To address this, we return to the six design themes expressed in new designs for professional learning.

Professional Development Is About Learning

The central message in professional development *as, in, at, outside of,* and *beyond* work is that the experience is centered in learning. Professional development that focuses on learning also conveys the message that the learner and his or her needs are primary considerations in the design, delivery, content, and assessment of professional learning experiences. When the design of professional development pays close attention to differences in learning styles, learner interests and preferences, and the learner's previous knowledge, it sends a powerful message to the teachers and principals. *I am an important part of the design of my professional learning. I am not just a passive recipient of new knowledge and skills.* Learner-centered professional development reinforces the message that professional development is about learning and growth, not activities and programs.

Every school has architecture for professional development that sends messages to teachers, administrators, school board members, and people in the community. As you think about the architecture for professional development in your school, what messages does it send about learning?

Professional Development Is Work

Like the design motifs repeated in many of Frank Lloyd Wright's buildings, professional learning as work is a recognizable feature in designs based on the new architecture of professional development. Professional learning communities legitimize professional learning as work by acknowledging its importance to high quality professional performance, to school improvement efforts, to individual development and growth, and to student learning. Each of these sends the message that ongoing professional learning is inextricably tied to professional work in schools. When schools create time for professional learning, build structures and provide resources to support it, and celebrate its importance through ceremonies, symbols, and cultural norms, they remind all educational stakeholders that professional development is an essential part of daily life in schools.

Professional Expertise Is a Journey, Not a Credential

New standards for professional licenses and the wisdom of practice indicate a growing recognition that the development of professional expertise is more than simply attaining a license to practice. Years ago, teachers and principals were able to complete their preservice preparation programs, apply for a license to practice, and then take a job and continue to practice until they had another professional career opportunity, quit, or retired. Receiving a license to practice was tantamount to being a professional. Today, the idea that a novice teacher or principal would have all of the requisite knowledge and skills needed for his or her career seems naive, to say the least.

When a teacher signs a contract to teach, he is also agreeing to a set of professional expectations that includes ongoing professional learning to continually update professional knowledge and skills, improve practice, and find ways to promote student learning. The new architecture of professional development taps into the richness of learning opportunities available to teachers and principals inside and outside of their schools. Professional expertise as a journey sends at least three key messages:

- Professional expertise is not a destination or license, it is an active dimension of professional work.
- Professional work and learning are inseparable and continuous.
- Teachers and principals have the support and resources of their work, their schools, and their colleagues as they journey toward greater levels professional expertise and personal and professional meaning.

Opportunities for Professional Learning Are Unbounded

The new architecture for professional development describes possibilities for creating and supporting professional learning opportunities for teachers and principals. Examples of professional development *as*, *in*, *at*, *outside of*, and *beyond* work send the message that professional learning and growth are not limited to scheduled inservice days or formalized activities called staff development. With appropriate support, resources, materials, and commitment, each of these venues offers potential learning opportunities to teachers and principals. The unboundedness of professional learning opportunities also suggests that individuals have significant autonomy, choice, and responsibility in determining their professional and personal growth.

Student Learning, Professional Development, and Organizational Mission Are Intimately Related

The complexity and hectic pace of professional work in schools often leaves career teachers and principals physically, emotionally, and intellectually exhausted at the end of the workday. Given that reality, calls for educators to learn new skills and meet new professional standards through ongoing professional development are often met with disbelief, silent resignation, or frustration. Professional development seems like something else added on to an already full workday. The new architecture for professional development recognizes these workplace realities and consequently looks within the routines and rhythms of teachers' and principals' ordinary work for professional learning opportunities. These *in situ* learning experiences bring work, learning, and school goals together helping to reduce feelings of fragmentation, overload, and incoherence. Professional learning is woven into the fabric of professional work and organizational priorities. This reinforces the message that professional development is work.

Professional Development Is About People, Not Programs and Activities

The new architecture for professional development is about building the personal and professional capacities of people. The primary organizers for this new architecture are professional development design, delivery, content, context, and outcomes. On occasion, we may fall into the trap of thinking that professional development in schools is only about refining technical skills, improving schools, and raising student test scores. These outcomes are certainly important objectives and very desirable outcomes. There is more to the new architecture for professional development than just-in-time training and advanced degrees. The new architecture for professional development at its core is a human endeavor, one that helps teachers and principals successfully negotiate the intersection of personal and professional dimensions of their lives as they connect with students and their colleagues. By bringing together the sometimes fragmented worlds of educators' work, life, and identity, the new architecture for professional development is about providing opportunities that give teachers and principals meaning and wholeness. Through the people it serves and celebrates, the new architecture for professional development is a language that communicates three essential messages—utilitas, firmitas, and venustas.

NOTE

1. O'Gorman, J. R. (1998). *ABC of architecture.* Philadelphia, PA: University of Pennsylvania Press, 87.

Index

Academic Employment Web site, 134
Accountability, educational outcomes and, 15-16
ACPA Web site, 134
Action, assessing levels of, 33
Action plan, professional development, 17
Action research:
    classroom, 83, 146-147, 156
    collaborative, 149
    teaching licensing and, 15
Adult learners, 79
    learning styles, 80
Alaska Web site, 134
Aldridge, B., 71, 76
Ambrose, 17, 19
American Federation of Teachers
    Web site, 119
American Speech-Language Hearing
    Association, 14
Analysis, 101
Appalachian Educational Laboratory
    (AEL) Web site, 103
Application, 101
Architecture of professional development,
    essential components of, 5-8, 153. *See
    also* Firmitas (structure), new
    architecture of professional
    development and; Utilitas (function),
    new architecture of professional
    development and; Venustas (beauty),
    new architecture of professional
    development and
Architecture of professional development,
    evaluating, 139-140, 151, 157. *See also*
    Assessment of professional
    development, reasons for;
    Professional development evaluation

Ashburton Centre Web site, 133
Assessment, professional work:
    professional development and, 100
    professional development "outside" of
        work and, 114-115
    school improvement plans and, 100
    student learning and, 100
    See also Assessment of professional
        development, reasons for
Assessment of professional development,
    reasons for, 142-143
    better information for planning, 142
    cognitive science, 142-143
    evaluating validity, 143
    professional learning and changes in
        practice, 143
    professional learning and
        compensation, 143
    return on investment, 142
    school improvement, 142
    See also Professional development
        evaluation
Assessment system, implementation of, 31
Association for Supervision and
    Curriculum Development Web site,
    17, 151
At-work professional development, 7
Authentic learning environments, 95
Authentic school communities, 97

Bambino, D., 85, 91
Barth, R., 41, 42, 50, 54, 55
Bay Area Writing Project (BAWP) Web
    site, 119
Becker, G., 71, 76
Beyond-work professional development, 7
Birman, B., 144, 152

Borko, H., 97, 105
Boud, D., 92, 93, 104
Boyer, E., 41, 42, 47, 54, 55
Bransford, J. D., 35, 39
Bredeson, P. V., 10, 11, 18, 30, 32, 38,
    39, 60, 62, 63, 65, 75, 76, 81, 90,
    95, 97, 104, 105, 106, 110, 114,
    121, 131, 135, 142, 152
Brown, A. L., 35, 39

California Subject Matter Projects (CSMPs)
    Web site, 119
Careerline Web site, 134
Central Park East Schools, 48
Chronicle of Higher Education
    Web site, 134
Coaching, 85
Cocking, R. C., 35, 39
Cognition, 44-45
    principles, 45
Collaborative inquiry, 32
    supporting, 31
Collaborative learning, 148
Collay, M., 41, 42, 54
Colleague consultation, 85
Collective reflection, 88
Collins, A. M., 44, 55
Communities:
    reculturing, xviii, xvi, xix
    restructuring, xviii, xvi, xix
    rethinking, xviii, xvi, xix
    schools as, 46-47
    See also Communities of practice;
        Community; Learning
        communities; Professional
        learning communities (PLCs)
Communities of practice, 79, 102-103
Community, 46
    concepts, 46
    responsive, 47
    See also Responsive school community
Conference. professional, 9
    attendance and teaching licensing, 15
Continuous learning, 89, 101
Contracts, negotiated, 32
Conventions, 112, 156
Corcoran, T. C., 142, 152
Council of Graduate Schools Web site, 119
Courage to Teach Teacher Formation
    Center Web site, 133
Culture, definition of, 31
Curriculum work teams, teaching
    licensing and, 15

Dade Academy for the Teaching Arts
    Web site, 120
Dade-Monroe Teacher Education Center
    (TEC) Web site, 120
Daily routines, ongoing professional
    learning in, 10
Danielson, C., 61, 76
Darling-Hammond, L., 13, 19, 108, 121
Deal, T., 31, 38
DeLoretto, L., 71, 76
Denver Zoo teacher travel program
    Web site, 133
Designing Effective Professional
    Development Web site, 17, 23, 37
Design themes, professional development.
    See Professional development design
    themes, new
Desimone, L., 144, 152
Dewey, J., 27, 85, 91, 129
Dialogue, 132
Distance learning, 96
Doyel, F., 71, 76
Dunlap, D., 41, 42, 54

Easton, L. B., 25, 38
Educational reform:
    investment in people and, 59
    professional development and, xv
Educational report cards, 15
Educational Resources Information Center
    Web site, 14
Education Week Web site, 89
Education World Web site, 103
Educators as Learners Web site, 53
Electronic connections, 96
Enloe, W., 41, 42, 54
Eraut, M., 144, 152
Evaluation, professional development.
    See Professional development
    evaluation
Evaluation of principals:
    formative, 100
    summative, 100
Evaluation of teachers:
    formative, 100
    summative, 100
Exloratorium Web site, 117
Exploring Middle School Reform
    Web site, 89

Fallingwater Web site, 3, 23
Feedback, 85
    continuous, 31

Firmitas (structure), new architecture of
    professional development and, 5, 6-7,
    140, 142, 151, 162
    learning opportunities content, 6
    learning opportunities delivery, 6
    learning opportunities design, 6
    Utilitas (function) and, 7
Force-field analysis, 86, 87
Fox, L. A., 61, 76
FREE Web site, 89
Fruth, M. J., 65, 76

Gagnon, G. W., Jr., 41, 42, 54
Gardner, J., 47, 55
Garet, M. S., 144, 152
Garrick, J., 92, 93, 104
Gerritz, W. H., 97, 105
Glatthorn, A. A., 61, 76
Glazer, S., 13, 19
Goldhammer, K., 71, 76
Gotham Writers' Workshop Web site, 133
"Grammar of schooling," 62, 65-66
    dynamic sameness and, 66
    nature of work and, 66
    professional development and, 66
Greeno, J. G., 44, 55
Griffin, N., 49, 55
Guskey, T. R., 97, 105, 143, 144, 145, 152
Guthrie, J. W., 97, 105

Habitat for Humanity Web site, 133
Handy, C., 16, 19
Hart, A. W., 62, 76
Hassel, E., 31, 38
Hawley, W. D., 23, 38
Heritage OnLine Continuing Education
    Web site, 119
Herman, R., 144, 152
Hirsch, S., 59, 75, 97, 104, 108, 121
Hoffer, Eric, 40
Hord, S. M., 51, 55

Ice Hotel Web site, 133
Incentives, teacher, 31
Individual self-study, 112
    transferring into team learning, 114
Informal learning at work, 78, 79. See also
    Professional development "in" work
In-school exchanges, 96
In-service training, 156
    limitations, 16
Institutes, 112, 113, 156
Integrity, 127

Interpretation, 101
Inward journeys, initiating, 132
In-work professional development, 7

Jefferson, Thomas, 27
Job-embedded learning, 78, 79-80, 92
    advantages, 80
    efficiencies, 81
    limitations, 85-86
    See also Professional development
        "in" work
Johansson, O., 95, 104
Joint Committee on Standards for
    Educational Evaluation, 143, 152
Joint work, 25, 32, 66
Joyce, B., 113, 121

Kasten, K. L., 65, 76
Kelley, C., 31, 38, 143, 152
Kilbourn, B., 78, 90
Kleiner, A., 51, 55, 116, 122
Knoster, 17, 19
Knowles, M., 79, 90
Komisar, P., 78, 90
Kottkamp, R. B., 82, 90
Kozol, J., 72, 76
Kretzman, J. P., 40, 54
Kruse, S., 63, 76

Leadership, strong school, 100
Learners, recognizing/honoring, 31
Learning, 44-46
Learning activities, showcasing, 31
Learning communities, 41, 50. See also
    Professional learning communities
    (PLCs)
Learning cultures:
    creating, 31-32, 33, 37
    thriving, 31
    See also Professional learning
        communities (PLCs)
Learning enriched schools, 66-67,
    97, 118
    common workplace elements, 98
    conceptual shifts, 67, 68, 75
    cultural shifts, 67, 70-72, 75
    structural shifts, 67, 68-70, 75
    See also Resources for learning-enriched
        schools; Workplace learning,
        optimal conditions for
Learning impoverished schools,
    49, 67, 71-72
    versus learning enriched schools, 69, 71

Learning-on-the-job opportunities,
    creating, 30-31
    providing incentives, 31
    providing materials/personnel/
        money, 30
    providing personal space, 30
    providing physical space to interact, 30
    providing time, 30-31
    removing inhibitors, 31
    restructuring time, 30
Learning outcomes,
    recognizing/honoring, 31
Learning principles, 9
    professional development in practice
        and, 45
"Learning to learn" skills, 113
Library Spot Web site, 103
License renewal, 10
    changes, 15
Licenses, 94
    advanced, 14
    probationary, 10, 14
    professional, 14, 94
Licensing requirements, new, 14-15, 60,
    160-161
    Wisconsin example, 60-61
    See also Action research projects;
        Conference attendance,
        professional; Curriculum work
        teams; Mentoring; Study groups
Lieberman, A., 36, 39, 108, 121
Little, J. W., 97, 105, 108, 121
Lortie, D., 61, 76
Louis, K. S., 63, 76

Mann, Horace, 27
Marsh, D. D., 97, 105
McGreal, T. L., 61, 76
McKnight, J. L., 40, 54
McLaughlin, M. W., 97, 105
Meetings, 96, 156
Meier, D., 48, 49, 55
Mental models, 50, 51
Mentoring, 32, 82, 85
    teaching licensing and, 15
Metz, M. H., 61, 76
Mid-Atlantic Laboratory for Student
    Success (LSS) Web site, 104
Mid-Continent Regional Educational
    Laboratory (McREL) Web site, 103
Miller, E., 71, 76
Miller, L., 36, 39
Mitchell, C., 41, 42, 50, 54, 55, 97, 105

Monk, D. H., 15, 19
Moore Johnson, S. 61, 76
Morgan, C., 71, 76

National Association of Elementary School
    Principals Web site, 119
National Association of School
    Psychologists, 14
National Association of Secondary School
    Principals Web site, 119
National Board of Professional Teaching
    Standards, board certification by, 14
National Center for Education Statistics,
    44, 55
National Center for Research on Teacher
    Learning (NCRTL) Web site, 119
National Commission on Teaching and
    America's Future (NCTAF), 13, 19
National Education Association:
    Foundation for the Improvement of
        Education Web site, 14, 121
    NEA Help from Web site, 75
National Foundation for the Improvement
    of Education, 64
National Library of Education (NLE)
    Web site, 89
National Staff Development Council,
    143, 152
    Web site, 14, 17, 23, 37, 119, 151
North Carolina Teacher Academy
    Web site, 120
North Central Regional Educational
    Laboratory (NCREL):
    guidebook, 22
    Web site, 17, 22, 53, 95, 103, 151
Northeast and Islands Laboratory at
    Brown University (LAB)
    Web site, 104
Northeast Regional Professional
    Development Center Web site, 17
Northwest Regional Educational
    Laboratory (NWREL) Web site, 103
Novick, R., 77, 90

Oberman, I., 97, 105
Odden, A., 31, 38, 143, 152
Off-site technology training, 148
O'Gorman, J. F., 5, 7, 18, 139,
    140, 152, 153, 162
On-site classes, 96
On-the-job learning, 78, 79-80, 81.
    See also Professional development
    "in" work

Oregon Educational Association (OEA)
    Web site, 121
Organizational culture, ongoing
    professional learning in, 10
Organizational development, professional
    development and, 10
Organizational learning, 41, 50-51. *See also*
    Mental models; Personal mastery;
    Shared vision; Systems thinking;
    Team learning
Organized abandonment, 41
Osterman, K. P., 82, 90
Outside-work professional
    development, 7

Pacific Region Educational Laboratory
    (PREL) Web site, 104
Palmer, P., 12, 18
Palmer, P. J., 123, 124, 125, 126, 127, 131,
    132, 134, 135
PBS Online Web site, 103
Peer coaching, 147, 156
    proponents, 147
Peer observation, 85
Peer support, 32
Personal actions, teachers', 29-30, 33, 37
Personal mastery, 50
Peterson, K. D., 31, 38
Plecki, M. L., 15, 19
Political support, developing, 32, 33, 37
Porter, A., 144, 152
Positive learning climate, 113
Postman, N., 27, 38
Prepackaged professional development
    activities, 23
Preservice training, 10
Principals:
    literature, 61-62
    professional development "as" work
        and, 73-74
Privacy/individualism, norms of, 62, 63
Professional, 42-44
    autonomy, 43-44, 161
    code of ethics, 43
    constraints, 44
    on-going reflection, 44
    openness to learning/improvement, 44
    professional self-assessment, 43
Professional development:
    effective, 14
    function of, 5-6
    primary purpose for teachers and
        principals, 36

Professional development, defining, 32,
    34-37, 88-89, 154
    creative/reflective engagement,
        34, 35-36, 88, 154
    improved practice, 34, 36-37, 89, 154
    learning opportunities, 34-35, 88, 154
Professional development, foundations
    for, 21-23, 154
    adequate resources, 28
    deep core values/commitment to
        learning, 21, 24-27, 37, 154
    durable attributes in levels of action,
        21, 24, 28-29, 37, 154
    moral purpose, 25, 27
    others' models and menus, 23
    site selection, 21-23
    valuing continuous learning, 24-25
    wide support of educators'
        work/professional growth, 21, 24,
        27-28, 37, 154
    See also Professional development,
        laying foundations for;
        Professional learning communities
        (PLCs)
Professional development, laying
    foundations for, 29-32
    continuous feedback, 31
    cultural actions, 29, 31-32, 33, 37
    incentives, 31
    personal actions, 29-30, 33, 37
    political actions, 29, 32, 33, 37
    removing barriers, 31
    structural actions, 29, 30-31, 33, 37
    See also Learning cultures
Professional development,
    traditional, 67
    criticisms, 60, 96-97
    problems, 60
    Professional development "at" work
        and, 95
Professional development activities,
    functions of, 36-37
    enhancement, 36-37
    establishment, 36
    organizational maintenance, 36
Professional development "as" work, 59,
    74-75, 155, 159, 161
    characteristics of professional work in
        schools and, 62-66
    expanded concept of professional
        development and, 60-61
    implications for administrators, 73-74
    implications for school boards, 74

implications for teachers, 72-73
major conceptual shifts and, 67, 68, 75
major cultural shifts and, 67, 70-72, 75
major structural shifts and, 67, 68-70, 75
Professional development "at" work,
    92-93, 156, 159, 161
    traditional staff development/
        in-service and, 95
    See also Distance learning; Electronic
        connections; In-school exchanges;
        Meetings; On-site classes; Teacher
        networks; Training; Workshops
Professional development "beyond" work,
    123-124, 133, 157, 159, 161
    avocational interests/activities, 124,
        125, 128-130, 133, 157
    broadening concept of professional
        development, 124-125
    communities of professional discourse
        and, 130
    individual identity and, 126-127
    inner creative/reflective activities, 124,
        125, 130-132, 133, 157
    professional learning community
        supports, 131
    school district supports, 130
    school supports, 130
    versus technique, 126-127
    See also Dialogue; Integrity; Inward
        journeys, initiating
Professional development delivery
    options, 112-113. See also
    Conventions; Individual self-study;
    Institutes; Staff retreats; Virtual
    networks
Professional development design features,
    contemporary, 4
Professional development designs:
    coherence of, 112
    integrative/connected, 112
Professional development design themes,
    new, 8-12, 159-162
    interrelatedness of student
        learning/professional
        development/organizational
        mission (theme five), xvi,
        8, 11-12, 161
    journey (theme three), xvi,
        8, 10, 160-161
    learning (theme one), xvi, 8, 9,
        159-160
    people not programs (theme six), xvi,
        8, 12, 162

unbounded opportunities (theme four),
    xvi, 8, 11, 161
work (theme two), xvi, 8, 9-10, 160
Professional development evaluation,
    143-144
    contexts of use and, 143, 144
    for judging/decision making, 144
    formative, 144
    for monitoring/adjusting/improving
        purposes, 144
    for planning purposes, 144
    Guskey's critical levels, 144-149, 157
    methods, 145, 157
    organizational context, 144
    organizational support/change, 147
    participants' learning, 146-147
    participants' reactions, 145-146
    participants' use of new
        knowledge/skills, 148
    policy context, 144
    practice context, 144
    purpose, 145, 157
    purposes, 143-144, 151
    school improvement planning and, 151
    student learning outcomes, 148-149
    summative, 144
    utility, 145, 157
    value, 145, 157
    See also Assessment of professional
        development, reasons for
Professional development evaluations,
    constructing, 149-151
    adequate support capacity, 149
    clear/client-centered purpose, 149, 150
    feasibility within school/districts'
        realities, 151
    reliable/credible methods for
        gathering/analyzing data, 151
    using data aligning with school goals,
        150, 151
    using data supporting professional
        learning, 150, 151
    using data supporting student
        learning, 151
Professional Development Guidelines
    (AFT), 13
Professional development in schools,
    importance of redesigning, 12-16
    accountability for education outcomes,
        15-16
    complex/demanding educator work,
        12-13
    new licensing regulations, 14-15

paradoxes in professional
    development, 16
school improvement, 13-14
Professional development "in" work, 78,
    89, 92-93, 155-156, 159, 161
    advantages, 80-81
    building connections, 80
    content, 79
    definition, 78-79
    empowerment, 79
    legitimization of practical
        knowledge, 80
    self-evaluation time, 80
    social support, 80
    structure of learning activity, 81
    See also Job-embedded learning
Professional development "in" work
    barriers, 87-88
    lack of interest, 88
    lack of skills, 88
    lack of time, 88
Professional development "in" work
    motivators, 86-87
    colleague support, 86, 87
    intrinsic value, 87
    personal enrichment, 87
    situated cognition/transfer, 86-87
    social interaction, 86, 87
Professional development "outside" of
    work, 106-108, 118, 156, 159, 161
Professional development "outside" of
    work, barriers/limitations to,
    108-110, 118
    in content dimension, 109
    in context dimension, 109-110
    in delivery dimension, 109
    in design dimension, 109
    in outcomes dimension, 110
Professional development "outside" of
    work, creating/supporting, 110-115
    content, 110, 111, 113, 118
    context, 110, 111, 113-114, 118
    delivery, 110, 111, 112, 118
    design, 110, 111, 112, 118
    outcomes, 110, 111, 114-115, 118
    See also "Learning to learn" skills;
        Professional development
        delivery options
Professional development paradigm,
    changing, 16-17, 154
    reculturing, 17, 154, 159
    resources needed, 17
    restructuring, 17, 154, 159

rethinking, 17, 154, 159
    See also Action plan, professional
        development
Professional development plans, 14
Professionalism, norms of, 32
Professional knowledge, sharing, 115-118
    developing norms for, 31
    See also Team learning
Professional learning:
    alignment, 116
    from colleagues, 23
    strong leadership, 100
Professional Learning Communities at
    Bruce-Monroe Elementary School
    Web site, 54
Professional learning communities (PLCs),
    xvi, 24-25, 41-51, 84, 114, 148, 156, 160
    administrator learning valued, 115
    celebrating learners/learning
        outcomes, 31
    collaborative inquiry in, 32
    commitment assessment tool, 26
    commitments to, 25
    consultation in, 25
    definitions, 41-42
    deprivatizing knowledge, 116
    deprivatizing practice, 31, 116
    developing norms for professional
        knowledge sharing, 31
    dialogue in, 24
    essence, 9, 117
    joint work in, 25, 32
    mentoring in, 32
    norms of professionalism, 32
    peer support in, 32
    recognizing/honoring
        learners/learning outcomes, 31
    reflective processes in, 25, 32
    shared learning in, 115
    showcasing learning activities, 31
    supporting collaborative
        inquiry/learning experiences, 31
    teacher learning valued, 115
Professional learning communities (PLCs),
    assessing attributes of, 51
    School Professional Staff Learning
        Community survey, 51
Professional learning communities (PLCs),
    creating, 48-51, 155
    clear/focused mission, 49
    coherent instructional programs, 49
    decision making structures, 49
    effective leadership, 49

parental support, 49
professional development, 49
strong professional culture, 49
Professional learning culture, professional
    learning "outside" work and, 114
Professional learning designs, confronting
    challenges in, 157-159
    paradoxes, 158
    school site condition, 158
    traditions/professional norms, 157
Professional learning "in" work, 81-85
    collaborative informal, 81, 82,
        83-84, 92, 156
    collaborative structured, 81, 82,
        84-85, 92, 156
    individual informal, 81, 82-83, 92, 156
    individual structured, 81, 82, 83, 92, 156
Professional practice, personalized, 62, 65
Professional work in schools,
        characteristics of, 62-66
    "grammar of schooling," 62, 65-66
    importance of psychic rewards, 62, 65
    norms of privacy/individualism, 62, 63
    paradoxes in practice, 62, 63-64
    personalized professional practice,
        62, 65
    uncertainties in teaching/leading,
        62-63
Psychic rewards, importance of, 62, 65
Putnam, R., 46, 55
Putman, R. T., 97, 105

Reeves, J. E., 62, 76
Reflection, 101
    in teaching, 82, 156
    on teaching, 82
Reflective conversations, 131
Reflective processes, 25, 32
Reitzug, U. C., 62, 76
Resnick, L. B., 44, 55
Resources for learning-enriched schools:
    adequate, 113, 114
    facilities, 98, 99
    materials, 98
    money, 98, 99
    support personnel, 98, 99
    time, 98-99
Responsive school community, 48. *See also*
    Professional learning communities
    (PLCs)
Roberts, C., 51, 55, 116, 122
Rosenholtz, S., 31, 38, 61, 66, 67, 76, 97, 105
Ross, R., 116, 122
Ross, R. D., 51, 55

Roth, G., 116, 122
Rubenson, K., 79, 90
Russell, Bill, 117

Sabbatical leaves, 113, 156
Sackney, L., 41, 42, 50, 54, 55, 97, 105
Schein, E. H., 30, 38
Schlecty, P. C., 36, 39
Schon, D. A., 80, 82, 90
School boards, professional development
    "as" work and, 72-73
School districts, number of, 44
School improvement:
    investment in people and, 59
    professional development and,
        10, 13-14
    student achievement and, 14
Schools:
    number of U.S., 44
    reculturing, xviii, xvi, xix
    restructuring, xviii, xvi, xix
    rethinking, xviii, xvi, xix
    struck versus thriving, 31-32
School structures, 99-100
    calendars, 99
    days, 99
    decision making, 100
    evaluation, 100
    instructional time, 99
    schedules, 99
    strong leadership, 100
Schutze, H. G., 79, 90
Scribner, J. P., 30, 38, 63, 76, 106, 121
Senge, P. M., 42, 44, 45, 50, 51, 55, 116, 117,
        122, 132, 135
Sergiovanni, T. J., 41, 42, 54
Shared vision, 50, 51
Shepheard, P., 3, 18
Showers, B., 113, 121
"Silos of separation," 11
Smith, B., 116, 122
Smith, B. J., 51, 55
Smylie, M. A., 59, 60, 75, 96, 104
SouthEastern Regional Vision for
    Education (SERVE) Web site, 104
Southwest Educational Development
    Council Web site, 53
Southwest Education Development
    Laboratory (SEDL) Web site, 104
Sparks, D., 59, 75, 97, 104, 108, 121
Speakers, 9
Specialization, 11
Staff development limitations, 16
Staff retreats, 112, 113, 131, 141

Standards, 15
Standards-based curricula, 15
Standards movement, 15
Stern, D., 79, 90, 97, 105
Strategic abandonment:
    capacity for, 52
    educational garage sale activity,
        52-53
Student learning, enhanced:
    professional development and, 10
Students, number of U.S., 44
Study/discussion groups, structured, 131
Study groups, xvii
    teaching licensing and, 15
Suk Yoon, K., 144, 152
Support structures, 113, 114
Sykes, G., 13, 19, 108, 121
Systems thinking, 50, 156

Taliesin Preservation Web site, 3
Teacher evaluation, professional
        development and, 61
    formative evaluation frameworks, 61
Teacher networks, 96
Teacher Professional Development
        Institute Web site, 54
Teachers:
    number of, 44
    professional development "as" work
        and, 72-73
Teachers@Work Web site, 134
TeacherServe Web site, 75, 120
Teacher skills, professional learning
        community:
    interpersonal capacity, 50
    organizational capacity, 50
    personal capacity, 50
Teacher study groups, 148-149
Teaching:
    acts of, 78-79, 81, 89
    as occupation, 78
    emotional, 12
    enterprise of, 78-79, 81, 89
    intellectual, 12
    literature, 61
    multiply disabled children, 13
    spiritual, 12
    uncertainties in, 62-63
    violent children, 13
    See also Teaching practice, paradoxes in
Teaching & Learning Academy
        Web site, 120
Teaching practice, paradoxes in,
        62, 63-64

meeting individual versus group
        needs, 63-64
    professional autonomy versus
        accountability measures, 64
    routine versus renewal, 64
Team learning, 50, 51, 66, 115-118
    complimentary efforts, 117
    displays/demonstrations
        example, 117
    mutual respect, 116
    opportunities to share/reflect/create
        meaning, 116
    poster sessions example, 118, 141
    strong cultures, 116
    training sessions example, 118
Team teaching, 84-85, 156
Tests, high-stakes, 15
Thinking outside the box, 5, 154
Thoreau, H. D., 20, 38
Time:
    as necessary resource, 98-99
    better-used, 99, 100
    common, 99, 100
    creating, 99-100
    freed-up, 99, 100
    purchased, 99, 100
    reorganizing, 99
    restructured, 99, 100
    school structures and, 99-100
Tobin, W., 62, 65, 76
Toffler, A., 11, 18
Training, 96
Training-of-trainer model, 118
Transfer of learning problems, 79
Tyack, D., 62, 65, 76

U.S. Department of Education
        Web site, 119
UNI Online Professional Development
        Web site, 119
Unions, 32
Unlearning, capacity for, 52
Unlearning organization, 41
Utilitas (function), new architecture of
        professional development and,
        5, 6, 140, 142, 151, 162
    client interests, 5-6
    client needs, 5-6
    client priorities, 5-6
    community building, 6
    enhance quality/impact of
        teaching/administration
        professions, 6
    firmitas (structure) and, 7

improve educator's quality of work
    life, 6
multiple beneficiaries, 6
organizational change facilitation, 6
student learning outcomes, 6
support local school improvement
    efforts, 6
See also Professional development,
    function of

Valli, L., 23, 38
Venustas (beauty), new architecture
    of professional development and,
    5, 7-8, 140-141, 142, 151, 162
    firmitas (structure) and, 8
    utilitas (function) and, 8
Virtual networks, 112, 131
Visiting Teacher Service Web site, 133
Vitruvius, definition of architecture
    by, 5, 140

Waller, W., 61, 76
Wenger, E., 46, 55, 102, 103, 105, 127, 134
Western Regional Educational Laboratory
    (WestEd) Web site, 103
Whitford, B. L., 36, 39
Wisconsin Department of Public
    Instruction, 15, 19, 60, 75

Withycombe, R., 71, 76
Wohlstetter, P., 49, 55
Wolcott, H. F., 62, 76
Workplace learning, 93
    advantages, 101-102
    disadvantages, 102
    in schools, 93-95
    research, 93, 94
Workplace learning, optimal conditions
    for, 97-101
    individual characteristics, 97, 98, 101
    resources, 97, 98-100
    school structures, 97, 98, 99-100
    social organization of school, 97-98
    team characteristics, 101
Workshops, xvii, 9, 96, 156
Wright, F. L., 3, 5, 8, 154, 159, 160
    Fallingwater, 3, 8, 23
    Guggenheim, 3, 8
    prairie school designs, 3, 4, 8, 16
    S. C. Johnson & Son Administration
        Building, 8
    Taliesin, 3, 159

Zhong, Guan, 12

**CORWIN
PRESS**

The Corwin Press logo—a raven striding across an open book—represents the happy union of courage and learning. We are a professional-level publisher of books and journals for K-12 educators, and we are committed to creating and providing resources that embody these qualities. Corwin's motto is "Success for All Learners."